ARROW FAMILY HANDBOOKS

THE FAMILY COOKBOOK

Arrow Family Handbooks

In any family's life there are bound to be major turning points, choices or moments of decision. Arrow Family Handbooks are designed to explore the alternatives and provide the information and practical advice you need.

Series editor: Mary Gilliatt

Other titles already published in this series:

Setting Up Home
A basic guide to what you need
Mary Gilliatt

Making Ends Meet
A practical guide to family finance
Elizabeth Gundrey

Time Out Together
A practical guide to family leisure out of doors
Caroline Mackinlay

Growing Up
A practical guide to adolescence for parents and children
Catherine Storr

The Family Cookbook

JUDITH LANCE

Illustrations by Arthur Robins

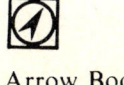

Arrow Books

The weights and measures throughout the
book are based on British Imperial Standards
and the nearest metric equivalent.

Arrow Books Ltd
3 Fitzroy Square, London W1

An imprint of the Hutchinson Publishing Group

London Melbourne Sydney Auckland
Wellington Johannesburg and agencies
throughout the world

First published by Arrow Books Ltd 1976
© Judith Lance 1976
Illustrations © Arthur Robins 1976

Made and printed in Great Britain
by litho by The Anchor Press Ltd
Tiptree, Essex

ISBN 0 09 913030 0

Contents

of Beef.   Corned Beef Hash.   Salmis of Chicken.   Fish Salad.
Curry Sauce.   Savoury Pancakes.   Croquettes.

Introduction

Some Thoughts About Breakfast and Packed Lunches. Yoghurt

Family cooking has a rather dull sound, as if it is all about nourishing and wholesome, rather than delicious and exciting food. French Provincial cooking doesn't sound dull, neither does Middle Eastern, Italian nor Chinese cooking, though they can all be used in family cooking. I am, however, only going to discuss straightforward meals in this book – the things we all do every day. I have not written about food for special occasions, special age groups or special diets. If you are trying to keep your family on a diet low in cholesterol, for instance, you may substitute polyunsaturated margarine for butter in any of the recipes. The result will not be the same, but this is a sacrifice that has to be made. I feel very strongly that family cooking offers something special both to the cook and the cooked *for*: cooking-with-love is more than just an exercise of skills and produces more than nourishment, and for the cook, it may be the only creative activity in a day filled with tedious tasks.

Above all, it is really a matter of how much time you have, because good cooking does take time – much more time than bad cooking. Doing anything well is seldom the quickest or easiest way of doing it. The day has only so many hours, so only cook the things you know you have time to do properly. And do what you like doing, because that is what you will do well.

Some Thoughts About Breakfast and Packed Lunches

I put these together because that is how they are for me, and for those mothers who send their children to school with homemade lunches. The couple of hours in the morning until everyone has left are very hectic and I have no magic formula to make them otherwise. There may be families who all leave at the same time and can all sit down to a peaceful breakfast together, but they must be rare. Leave gracious living for weekend breakfasts and on week days just go as fast as you can. However early you might seem to be, someone invariably loses his cap, homework book or temper before you get them all on their way.

It doesn't matter if breakfast is only fruit, toast and coffee, or cereal and coffee, for this is a meal that doesn't seem to interest children. Let them have what they want; it will be less exhausting for you than trying to force everyone to have a traditional start to the day and no one really needs an egg every morning. My five children have five different breakfasts, and although this sounds a nuisance, it is quicker in the long run and everything is eaten. If you have an early waker who wants to make her own instant porridge at 6 a.m., let her do it if she doesn't wake everyone else. So one eats muesli, one boils an egg and one has yoghurt. Try not to worry if some will eat only one piece of toast, they will almost certainly make up for it at some other meal which suits them.

I exclude from these remarks, of course, children up to about three years old. Whatever dieticians tell us (I know, because I am one) mothers know that many babies and small children will *not* select or accept an adequate diet for themselves, and would starve to death before your very eyes if you didn't coax and cajole. So go ahead, persuade the child who needs it, and add to the persuasion beautifully prepared food of even the simplest kind.

Big bowls of yoghurt in the refrigerator are our most useful all-round food. Yoghurt is formed by bacterial action so the first time you make it you will need to buy a small carton of the commercial kind as a starter. After your first batch, just put a little aside for the next. It keeps for at least a week, or can be frozen for as long as you like.

Yoghurt

1½ lb (675 g) powdered skim milk ½ pint (3 dl) boiling water
1½ pints (1 litre) cold water 1 pint (6 dl) tepid water
15 oz (425 g) tin evaporated milk 2 tablespoons sugar
½ teaspoon powdered gelatine 3 tablespoons yoghurt

Preheat oven to 275°F, 140°C or Gas No. 1

Dissolve the powdered skim milk in the cold water. Add the tin of evaporated milk. Dissolve the gelatine in the boiling water and add this to the milk mixture, together with the tepid water, in which you have dissolved the sugar. Stir in the yoghurt. Put in an ovenproof dish. Turn off the oven, put in the yoghurt, covered with a cloth, and leave it there all night with the door shut.

Add any sort of sweetened, stewed, fruit to it. Apricots, prunes and spiced apple are all good.

While all this breakfasting is in progress, you are probably making sandwiches. They are so much easier than any other form of packed lunch and there are very few children who do not love them if the bread is fresh. Bread is a beautiful and nutritious food which should be treated well, so buy your sandwich bread (sliced) and put it straight in the freezer of your refrigerator. If you have the space, get into the habit of *always* keeping your bread frozen unless you are going to heat it and

10   eat it hot. There is no need to thaw it to make sandwiches. Just about anything mixed with homemade mayonnaise is fine – tuna, egg, leftover chopped-up chicken or meat; and all are better with shredded lettuce in them. Do the same thing with bread rolls. Freeze them as soon as you get them home – a bread knife will saw through them frozen in the morning. Fill them, and they will thaw by lunchtime.

Most days I try to put some tiny surprise thing in the lunches for the smaller children, and for the bigger ones as well for that matter, small packets of chips or dried fruit, whatever you can think of.

All of us have the child who will *only* eat peanut butter sandwiches, and *only* if they are cut in the shape of a house. I just go ahead and make them. I doubt if eating food you don't like is character building. The leaves on the dahlias outside our dining-room window when I was a child, glisten in my mind to this day with the milk and lemon sago my sisters and I hurriedly emptied on them.

1. Stocks, Soups and Sauces

It seems to be impossible to make soups or sauces calling for stock with anything other than the real thing, although stock cubes can be used successfully if stock is needed when stewing meat or vegetables, when the strong flavour of the main ingredient is enough to overcome the otherwise characteristic flavour of the cube. I know that carefully prepared stocks are essential to many fine dishes, but in the context of family cooking I feel it is an extravagance to buy ingredients specifically for stock. I never do it, but I always like to have some frozen fish and chicken stock in the freezer for sauces or soup. I don't seem to need meat stock very often; when making a sauce such as a velouté for a meat dish, there is usually the cooking liquid from the meat to use. Stock can, of course, be made with veal and beef bones, without meat.

STOCKS

Chicken Stock

If you use frozen roasting chickens and poach them instead of roasting them, they are not only better for made-up chicken dishes and cold chicken, but you have the added dividend of a pot of chicken stock. (See page 28, for cooking the chickens for chicken pie.) If you have room to freeze the stock, the next time you cook a chicken you can cook it *in* the stock; the resulting liquid will be richer still and the chicken better as well.

Fish Stock

Always ask for the bones and head when you have a fish filleted. Making fish stock is not particularly pleasant, but if you make it in a spare moment and then freeze it, you will be much more likely to make an exquisite sauce at some other time. There are some fish dishes which may not provide any stock (a whole baked fish, some fish soufflés and mousses, or any dish for which you have bought ready filleted fish) but they become really delicious with the addition of a beautiful fish sauce.

Cooking time: 30 minutes
2 pints (generous 1 litre) water (or to cover the fish)
the heads and bones of one or two good fish
2 tablespoons vinegar or a glass of dry white wine

1 peeled onion
1 slice lemon
salt, peppercorns
other herbs if you wish – parsley, fennel, thyme or bay
Simmer uncovered for 30 minutes. Strain.

This is used as the basis of fish soups or a fish velouté, and can be boiled down to make the concentrated fish fumet which is the basis of the exquisite white wine sauce, a sort of fish hollandaise.

SOUPS

The following recipes are for very simple soups, some using chicken stock, most using one main vegetable. But simple does not mean humble, each is very good and an excellent start to a dinner party. They are, for the most part, simple, because few of us have the time or inclination for the lengthy chopping that went into the hearty soups our mothers made, unless we have families who are prepared to accept soup as a full meal. These are lighter soups, of clearly defined flavour, and my particular favourites.

Mushroom Soup
Serves 8.   Cooking time: 25 minutes

12 oz (350 g) mushrooms	1¾ pints (10½ dl) light chicken
2 oz (50 g) butter	stock
1 clove garlic	salt and pepper
2 tablespoons chopped parsley	pinch ground nutmeg
1 thick slice of bread	¼ pint (1½ dl) single cream

Wipe and chop the mushrooms. Chop garlic. Soak the bread in a little stock. Melt the butter in a saucepan, add the mushrooms and cook gently for 2–3 minutes, then add the chopped garlic, a tablespoon of chopped parsley, salt, freshly ground pepper and a pinch of nutmeg and continue cooking for a few minutes. Be careful with the salt and pepper as your stock will, no doubt, be seasoned already. Squeeze the moisture out of the bread and mix the bread into the mushrooms. Add the rest of the stock, bring up to the boil and simmer for 15 minutes, or until the mushrooms are soft. Draw the pan off the heat. Rub the soup through a sieve or Mouli or purée in a blender. Do not make it too smooth. Return to the pan, check seasoning and reheat. Before serving add the cream and the other tablespoon of chopped parsley.

Carrot Soup

Serves 8. Cooking time: approximately 30 minutes

1 lb (450 g) fresh young carrots
1 onion
2 oz (50 g) butter
1 clove garlic
2 tablespoons chopped parsley

1 thick slice of bread
1¾ pints (10½ dl) light chicken stock
salt and pepper
pinch nutmeg

Soak the bread in a little stock. Scrape and slice the carrots. Peel and finely slice the onion. Melt the butter in a saucepan, add the prepared vegetables and cook gently for several minutes. Chop the garlic and then add it, together with 1 tablespoon of chopped parsley, salt, freshly ground pepper and a pinch of nutmeg and continue cooking for a few minutes. Squeeze the moisture out of the bread and mix it into the mixture in the pan. Add the rest of the stock and bring up to the boil, then simmer gently until the vegetables are tender. Draw the pan off the heat. Rub the soup through a sieve or Mouli or purée in the blender. Return the soup to the pan, check seasoning, and reheat. Sprinkle with the other tablespoon of parsley just before serving. This soup can also be thickened with potatoes instead of bread. In this case add a few sliced potatoes to the carrots and onion at the beginning of the recipe. Or if you wish to thicken it with rice, add a handful of rice to the stock. If, on the other hand, you would rather have a thinner soup, dilute it with a little extra stock.

Spinach Soup

Serves 8.   Cooking time: 20–30 minutes

8 handfuls of fresh spinach *or*
2 lb (1 kg) packet of frozen
  spinach
1 onion
2 oz (50 kg) butter
1 clove garlic

2 tablespoons chopped
  parsley
1¾ pints (10½ dl) light chicken
  stock
salt and pepper
pinch nutmeg
¼ pint (1½ dl) single cream

Peel and finely slice the onion. Chop the garlic. Melt the butter in a saucepan, add the onion and spinach and cook gently for several minutes, then add the garlic, 1 tablespoon of chopped parsley, salt, freshly ground pepper and a pinch of nutmeg and continue cooking for a few minutes. Add the stock, bring up to the boil, then simmer gently until the vegetables are tender. Draw the pan off the heat. Rub the soup through a sieve or Mouli or purée in a blender. Return the soup to the pan, check seasoning and reheat. Before serving add the cream and sprinkle over the chopped parsley.

Pea Soup

Serves 8.   Cooking time: 25–30 minutes

Do not be deceived by the simplicity of this recipe. If the peas are young and fresh (and it's not worth making it otherwise) it is one of the most delicious dishes on earth.

1¾ lb (550 g) peas
1 lettuce heart
4 oz (100 g) butter

1¾ pints (10½ dl) water
2 teaspoons salt
1 teaspoon sugar

Clean and shred the lettuce. Pod the peas. Melt butter, add peas, lettuce, sugar and salt and cook gently in a covered saucepan for 10 minutes, until the peas are thoroughly soaked with butter. Add the water and cook over moderate heat until the peas are quite tender. Rub the soup through a sieve or Mouli or purée in a blender. Return the soup to the pan, reheat, check seasoning.

Tomato Soup

Serves 6–8.   Cooking time: 15 minutes. Allow several hours to chill

2 lb (1 kg) ripe tomatoes	2 oz (50 g) diced ham
1 teaspoon salt	4 oz (100 g) diced cucumber
1 teaspoon sugar	finely chopped parsley
1 tablespoon lemon juice	$\frac{1}{8}$–$\frac{1}{4}$ pint ($\frac{3}{4}$ dl–$1\frac{1}{2}$ dl) single
1 teaspoon onion juice	cream

Purée the raw tomatoes and strain. Add the salt, sugar, lemon juice and onion juice, tasting as you do and varying the amounts if needed. Chill for several hours. Add the ham, cucumber and cream just before serving and sprinkle with parsley.

Vichysoisse

Serves 6–8.   Cooking time: 40 minutes. Allow several hours to chill

This soup has to be very smooth, and is supposed to be put through one sieve and then a finer one. I used to find this rather hard work before I had a blender, which makes it all very easy.

4 leeks	1 stalk celery
1 onion	2 tablespoons finely chopped
2 medium-sized potatoes	chives
2 oz (50 g) butter	1 tablespoon chopped parsley
2 pints (12 dl) chicken stock	salt and pepper
	$\frac{1}{2}$ pint (3 dl) single cream

Trim, clean and finely slice the leeks. Peel and chop the onion. Melt the butter in a saucepan and gently fry the leeks and onion, covered with a lid, until they are soft, but not brown. Peel and finely slice the potatoes. Shred the celery. Add everything else except the cream and chives and bring to the boil. Simmer until the potatoes are tender. Rub the soup through a fine sieve or Mouli, or purée in a blender. When cool, stir in the cream, check seasoning and chill. Serve with finely chopped chives. Vichysoisre can be made with water instead of chicken stock.

Cold cucumber soup can be made in the same way.

Peel 4 cucumbers and de-seed. Slice thinly, blanch for 2 minutes and drain. Then continue as for Vichysoisse.

Fish Soup
Serves 10–12.   Cooking time:1¼ hours

This is a whole lunch soup. The most you would need after it would be some cheese or salad. The stock is made first. It doesn't take long, but if you make it well beforehand, you may enjoy eating it more.

3 good-sized fish, about 2 lb (1 kg) each, or a number of
    smaller fish, preferably different varieties.
1 lb (450 g) tomatoes
½ lb (225 g) onions
1 bay leaf
½ teaspoon thyme
large pinch saffron
fennel
few sprigs parsley as well as some extra chopped parsley
2 or 3 cloves garlic
1 tablespoon flour
olive oil for frying
salt and pepper

Have the fish filleted, use the heads, bones and trimmings for the stock. Cut the fillets into 2-inch (4 cm) slices to add later. Peel and slice the onions and sauté them in olive oil until soft. Sprinkle with a tablespoon of flour while stirring. Crush the garlic and add this to the onions, together with the chopped tomatoes, bay leaf, thyme, saffron, fennel (if available) and a few sprigs of parsley. Season with salt and pepper. Add the fish heads, bones and trimmings, cover with water (about 3 pints (18 dl)). Boil fairly hard, uncovered, for 40 minutes.

Strain, pushing through all the liquid you can. Put out the rubbish straight away, it's so depressing. Return the broth to the rinsed-out saucepan or soup pot. Correct seasoning. Now all you have to do is add the pieces of fish to cook for 5–10 minutes just before serving. Add some chopped parsley and serve with garlic bread.

SAUCES

The number and complexity of sauces it is possible to make always seems alarming, but many of them are really the simple sauces we all make without a thought, with some extra ingredient and a fancy name. A white sauce, mayonnaise, French dressing and béarnaise sauce can be adapted in many different ways. They all have a place in family cooking, because a sauce can make an otherwise ordinary meal special, or a beautiful dinner from leftovers.

Ordinary White Sauce
Makes ¾ pint. Cooking time: 10–40 minutes

1 oz (25 g) plain flour   ¾ pint (4½ dl) hot milk
1 oz (25 g) butter or margarine   salt and pepper

Melt the butter over low heat and stir in the flour. Cook for a few minutes. In another saucepan bring the milk almost to the boil and add it all at once. Beat hard. If you use cold milk, take the pan off the stove and add the milk, little by little, stirring or whisking all the time. Then in both cases season the sauce and bring it to the boil still stirring. Another half an hour's gentle cooking improves all white sauces, making them more satiny, but it is not absolutely necessary.

For a thick white sauce, for use in binding leftovers or for a sauce to be thinned down later, use only ½ pint (3 dl) of liquid.

Béchamel Sauce
Makes ¾ pint (4½ dl).   Cooking time: 10–40 minutes

1 oz (25 g) plain flour   ½ onion stuck with a clove
1 oz (25 g) butter or margarine   1 bay leaf
¾ pint (4½ dl) milk   6 peppercorns
salt and pepper

This is exactly the same as an ordinary white sauce, except that you add the bay leaf, onion and peppercorns to the milk before bringing it to the boil. Once heated take it off the stove and leave it to infuse for 10 minutes. Strain the milk and continue as for a white sauce.

Sauce Mornay
Makes ¾ pint (4½ dl).   Cooking time: 10–40 minutes

Is béchamel with cheese added, as everyone who has ever made macaroni cheese on Sunday night, knows. Cook the sauce and at the end add 4 oz (100 g) of grated cheese. It should be Parmesan and Gruyère, but that will not stop me, nor anyone else, from using up whatever suitable cheese they have. Continue cooking only long enough to melt the cheese. For vegetables, pasta, fish au gratin.

Velouté Sauce
Makes ½ pint (3 dl).   Cooking time: 10–40 minutes

1 oz (25 g) plain flour   squeeze of lemon juice
1 oz (25 g) butter or margarine   ¾ pint (4½ dl) hot stock
salt and pepper

This uses the same method as the basic white sauce, but uses an appropriate stock instead of the milk. Proceed as for a white sauce. At the moment of seasoning add the squeeze of lemon juice.

This is either thick béchamel or a velouté thinned down with cream and a few drops of lemon juice at the end of cooking. This is a more liquid sauce and is particularly good with any leftovers you want to serve au gratin. That is, mixed with the sauce and reheated in the oven, with cheese or breadcrumbs on top, until crisp and brown. Add parsley and tarragon for chicken; other herbs according to the dish you are making.

Sauce Soubise
Makes ½ pint (3 dl).   Cooking time: 25–30 minutes

1½ oz (37 g) butter
1 oz (25 g) plain flour
½ lb (225 g) onions

½ pint (3 dl) hot stock
pinch ground nutmeg
¼ pint (1½ dl) single cream (optional)

Peel and finely slice the onions. Melt the butter and fry the onions gently. Do not let them brown. Add the flour and cook for a few minutes, stirring all the time. Pour in the stock a little at a time and continue stirring. Bring up to the boil. Sieve the sauce, pressing it out well. Add cream if liked. Flavour it with a little nutmeg before serving. If you roast veal in a covered pan, use the juice from the cooking to make a beautiful sauce soubise to serve with it.

Sauce Robert

This can be made in the same way as a sauce soubise, but use no cream. After having added the stock, stir in 1 teaspoon of French mustard and 1 tablespoon of vinegar. Especially good with grilled pork chops, and try it with hamburgers.

Mayonnaise
Makes ½ pint (3 dl).   Time taken: 15–20 minutes

½ pint (3 dl) olive oil
2 egg yolks or even 3
pinch dry mustard
salt and freshly milled pepper

3 teaspoons lemon juice or white wine vinegar
1 tablespoon boiling water

Have everything at room temperature and warm the bowl. Mayonnaise is best made with a wire whisk, but can be made with any beater. Beat the egg yolks, mustard, salt and pepper and 1 teaspoon of vinegar or lemon juice very well before you begin to add the oil. Add the oil one teaspoon at a time, beating hard after each addition. You should add it drop by drop, but it is not really necessary, particularly if you have used 3 egg yolks. Once it has thickened, you can add the oil more quickly. When it gets too stiff, add another teaspoon of vinegar or lemon. Finally add the last of the vinegar or lemon (first taste and see if you feel it needs more or less) and then the boiling water. It's terribly tiring, and if it curdles (which happens if you pour the oil too fast or if the eggs and oil are at a different temperature) you must start again and beat the curdled mixture very gradually into another well-beaten yolk.

MAYONNAISE VARIATIONS

Aïoli
Makes ½ pint (3 dl).   Time taken: 20 minutes

3 or 4 cloves of garlic
½ pint (3 dl) olive oil
2 egg yolks
pinch dry mustard

salt and freshly milled pepper
2 teaspoons lemon juice or
  white wine vinegar
1 tablespoon boiling water

Pound the cloves of garlic in a pestle and mortar. Proceed as for mayonnaise, adding the garlic to the egg yolks, before the oil is poured in. Serve with boiled fish, hardboiled eggs, and boiled potatoes. Also used in bourride (see page 27).

Sauce Verte
Makes ½ pint (3 dl).   Time taken: 30 minutes

½ pint (3 dl) mayonnaise
1 teaspoon French mustard
2 handfuls fresh spinach, *or* 1 small packet frozen spinach
1 tablespoon each of chopped watercress, parsley, chervil and
  tarragon.

Make a green purée by blanching the spinach, watercress and herbs in boiling water for a few minutes. Drain very well, then pound and push them through a sieve. Drain again if necessary. The resulting *dry* purée is mixed with the mayonnaise. Delicious with cold salmon, salmon, trout, any cold poached fish, peeled prawns or hard-boiled eggs.

Sauce Rémoulade
Makes ½ pint.   Time taken: 15–20 minutes

To ½ pint (3 dl) of mayonnaise add:
2 teaspoons French mustard
1 tablespoon each of gherkins, capers, parsley, and chervil all chopped
½ teaspoon anchovy sauce or essence, or 2 or 3 pounded anchovy fillets

For prawns and salmon, but good with hot meats too.

Sauce Tartare
Makes ½ pint (3 dl).   Time taken: 15–20 minutes

½ pint (3 dl) mayonnaise
1 rounded dessertspoon each gherkins, capers, chives, parsley, all finely chopped, together with the finely chopped peel of ½ lemon.

Add the ingredients to the mayonnaise. Good with cold meats and fish, especially fried fish.

French Dressing
Makes just under ¼ pint (1½ dl).   Time taken: 5 minutes

salt and freshly milled pepper   6 tablespoons olive oil
pinch dry mustard   2 tablespoons white wine
vinegar

Combine all ingredients and mix well. I use so much that I always have some made up in a screw-top jar, with a few cloves of garlic sitting in it. Shake it up well before using.

Sauce Ravigote
Makes ½ pint (3 dl). Time taken: 20 minutes

1 small onion or shallot, chopped	2 teaspoons chopped chervil
	½ teaspoon chopped tarragon
1 tablespoon chopped capers	1 teaspoon chopped chives
1 teaspoon chopped parsley	½ pint (3 dl) French dressing

Mix up everything well. Particularly for cold meats. Good for using up cold roast beef.

Béarnaise Sauce
Makes 1 pint (6 dl). Cooking time: 40 minutes

9 tablespoons dry, white wine
4 tablespoons tarragon vinegar or white wine vinegar, plus 1 handful of fresh or dried tarragon
1 medium onion, chopped
1 handful chopped parsley
small nut butter
6 egg yolks
salt and freshly milled pepper
8 oz (225 g) butter (soft)

Simmer together the wine, vinegar, parsley, tarragon, onion, salt and pepper and nut of butter until the liquid is reduced by at least half. It will take about 30 minutes. Remove from heat. Strain out the onion and herbs. This liquid is the basis of the sauce and by varying this, you can make other sauces. Still off the heat add the egg yolks, one by one, beating them in very well. Now over gentle heat add the softened butter piece by piece, whisking all the time with an egg beater or wire whisk (I like a small whisk best), and putting your finger in to see that it's not getting too hot. If the eggs should start to set, get it off the stove and beat like mad and it will probably be all right. As you add the butter it will increase in volume and finish up looking like softly beaten cream. Add a little more very finely chopped tarragon at the end if you like.

If you cannot face the thought of making the sauce while your family or friends wait for it, you can make it before it is needed, and keep it warmish beside the stove, or over warm water. It is delicious with beef, or if you make it with mint instead of tarragon, it is good with lamb.

BÉARNAISE VARIATIONS

Sauce Choron

This is béarnaise flavoured with tomato purée. Stir it in at the end. For grilled meat or fish dishes.

Hollandaise Sauce
Makes: see below.   Cooling time: 15 minutes

¼ pint (1½ dl) dry white wine (or ½ vinegar and ½ water)
salt and freshly milled pepper
2 chopped shallots
2 egg yolks
few drops lemon juice
4 oz (100 g) butter (soft)

Simmer the liquids, salt, pepper and shallots over a gentle heat until you are left with 2 tablespoons. Take off the heat and strain. Beat in the egg yolks, one by one. Now over gentle heat add the softened butter, piece by piece, whisking all the time with an egg beater or wire whisk. Put your finger in to see that it's not getting too hot. When the sauce has thickened add a few drops of lemon juice. If it *does* start to curdle, suspend operations, break another yolk into a bowl and add the curdled sauce bit by bit until it amalgamates again. This is not quite as bland as the usual hollandaise. Very good with vegetables or poached fish or eggs. Serve warm.

This is enough for a separate vegetable dish for 4 people.

Sauce Mousseline

Makes ½ pint (3 dl).   Cooking time: 10 minutes

¼ pint (1½ dl) cream
½ pint (3 dl) hollandaise

Fold in some whipped cream at the last moment. A very delicate sauce for fish or vegetables.

White Wine Sauce for Fish

Serves 8 if using for a fish soufflé.   Cooking time: 15 minutes

fish stock (see page 12) made   4 oz (100 g) butter (soft)
   with white wine   squeeze of lemon juice
2 egg yolks

Boil down the fish stock to 2 tablespoons of concentrated fish fumet. Withdraw from heat. Strain, and still off the heat, beat in the egg yolks one by one. Now over gentle heat add the softened butter, piece by piece, whisking all the time. Finish off by adding a squeeze of lemon juice. If you are poaching fish in the oven, with white wine and some herbs, lift the fish out when it is cooked and boil down the poaching liquid to start off the sauce. Delicious with a fish soufflé or a baked fish.

2. Main Dishes for Dinner

I would love to start this chapter with one of those well-worn but still very impressive sentences: decide on your dinner menu according to whatever is freshest and the best value in the markets in the morning. You would then have a lovely picture of colourful open-air markets in say, provincial France, and think how satisfying it must be to be that sort of housewife. Perhaps some of you are – I hope so. For most of us, however, what we cook for dinner is inevitably influenced by time, more specifically by how much time we are likely to have to cook in the evening: lots, some, or none. No one needs advice for the 'lots of time' days, they happen so seldom. For the 'some time' days, it is useful to have dishes which can be prepared in two stages. For example, chicken pie or steak and kidney pie, which you can prepare all except for baking the pastry; or dishes like sauerbraten, which need a bit of time at the end for the dumplings and sauce. I have clearly marked these recipes, divided into their two stages. This is the time, as well, for meats or fish that take a short time to cook. For the 'no time' days, here are some recipes which are completely prepared beforehand and just need heating up when you come in. Vegetables, if any, would have to be prepared beforehand too. So 'no time' here, only means time at some other hour or on another day whichever is the more convenient. I like to cook straight after breakfast if I can, while the kitchen is still in a mess. This gives me time to cook, chill and take the fat off foods easily.

A 'SOME TIME' RECIPE
Bourride

Serves 6.   Cooking time: first stage: 35 minutes. Second stage 35–40 minutes

This recipe is included because, firstly, a number of my children are firm non-fish eaters, and the first time I made bourride they joined the others in actually *fighting* over who should have the last pieces, and secondly, it can be made with just about any sort of fish, or a combination of several. Basically it consists of fish fillets poached in fish stock, served on fried bread with lots of delicious sauce poured over it, accompanied by boiled potatoes. The sauce is made by mixing the stock in which the fish was cooked with aïoli (garlic flavoured mayonnaise, page 21).

6 thick fillets of fish
heads and bones of the fish
1 onion
salt
freshly milled pepper
1 slice of lemon
1 bay leaf

1 pint (6 dl) water
1 tablespoon white wine vinegar
6 slices of bread
3 lb (1½ kg) new potatoes
oil for frying
chopped parsley

3 cloves garlic

½ pint (3 dl) olive oil

2 egg yolks

pinch dry mustard

salt and freshly milled pepper

2 teaspoons lemon juice or white wine vinegar

First stage (*fish stock*)

Ask the fishmonger to fillet the fish and to give you the heads and bones. Peel and slice the onion. Put the heads and bones of the fish, the onion, lemon, bay leaf, water and vinegar into a saucepan with a seasoning of salt and pepper. Bring to the boil. Simmer for 30 minutes, strain. Make Aïoli (see page 21).

Second stage

Poach your fish fillets gently in the stock until they are done. While the fish is cooking, boil the new potatoes and fry the slices of bread in oil. Keep them warm. Remove the fish from the stock and keep it warm. Boil the stock down quickly to reduce it by half. Take the Aïoli, put it in a basin, and strain in the hot reduced stock until you have a creamy sauce. Stir all the time you are doing this. Put the fried bread on a big serving dish, the fish on top of it, covered with sauce and the potatoes round the edge. Sprinkle chopped parsley over the top.

A 'SOME TIME' RECIPE

Chicken Pie

Serves 6–8.   Cooking time: first stage: 1½ hours. Second stage 40 minutes

1 3 lb (1½ kg) chicken

1 onion

4 sticks celery

2 bay leaves

6 peppercorns

salt

4 carrots

1 lb (450 g) peas

4 medium white onions

For the Sauce
2 oz (50 kg) butter
2 oz (50 g) flour
1 pint (6 dl) stock

For the Pastry
6 oz (150 g) self-raising flour
4 oz (100 g) margarine
salt
3–4 tablespoons cold milk

First stage

Put the chicken into a saucepan in which it should just fit. Cover with water, add the peeled onion, 1 stick of celery, bay leaves, peppercorns and salt. Bring to the boil, skim, then simmer gently for $\frac{3}{4}$–1 hour (stick a skewer in the thigh and see if it runs clear – do not overcook). Partly cool in the stock. Discard skin and take all the meat off the bones and cut into fairly large pieces. If you have time, boil the stock down a bit with the bones in it. Cool the stock then chill and take the fat off it. If you do this, the cooking of the chicken should be done the night before. While the chicken is cooking, make the pastry.

Sift the ingredients. Cut margarine to size of small peas. Rub the margarine into the flour and salt with the fingertips until the mixture is like fine breadcrumbs. Pour in the milk, all at once, and mix into a pliable dough. Knead on a floured board. Wrap in polythene and put in the refrigerator.

Scrape and slice the carrots. Wash and slice 3 sticks of celery. Cut the white onions in quarters. Pod peas, unless you are using frozen. Once the chicken is cooked and the stock cool, cook the vegetables in the chicken stock. Do not overcook; the vegetables should be firm. Drain. *Keep this vegetable/ chicken stock for the sauce.*

Second stage

Take pastry out of the refrigerator, so that it regains room temperature. You *could* make the sauce in the first stage, but it's better to do it at the last moment. Melt butter in a saucepan, add flour and cook together for a couple of minutes, then add the stock in which you cooked the vegetables. Cook gently, stirring all the time. Make quite a lot of sauce, as this is a big pie and must not be dry. Mix the sauce with the chicken and vegetables and put it all in a buttered pie dish.

30   Roll out the pastry, not too thinly. Line the edge of the dish with pastry trimmings. Damp with water. Cover pie with pastry and make a small slit in the top. Make roses with pastry scraps – one for each member of the family. Glaze with milk. Bake at (425°F, 220°C, Gas 6–7) for 25–30 minutes.

A 'SOME TIME' RECIPE

Steak and Kidney Pie
Serves 6–8. Cooking time: first stage: 2 hours. Second stage 30 minutes

2 lb (1 kg) stewing steak	salt and freshly ground pepper
2 lambs kidneys	pinch nutmeg
1 onion	seasoned flour
2 small tomatoes	6 oz (150 g) pastry (see page 29)
2 bacon rashers	1 oz (25 g) fat for frying

First stage

Cut the steak up into 1-inch (2 cm) pieces. Snip core from kidneys and cut up. Peel and chop onion. Nick the skins of the tomatoes and plunge them in boiling water. Take out, peel and chop. Cut up bacon rashers. Roll meat in seasoned flour and fry until browned all over. Put all the ingredients into a saucepan and barely cover with water. Bring to the boil and simmer, covered, for 2 hours. Pour into a pie dish and cool.

Make pastry as for chicken pie (previous page). Leave it in the refrigerator.

Second stage

Take pastry out of refrigerator. Wait until it has regained room temperature. Roll it out, not too thinly. Line the edge of the dish with pastry trimmings. Damp with water. Cover pie with pastry and make a small slit in the top. Make roses with pastry scraps – one for each of the family. Glaze with milk. Bake at (425°F, 220°C, Gas 6–7) for 25–30 minutes.

Both these pies are good with mashed potatoes, and for the steak and kidney pie serve a green vegetable as well.

Sauerbraten

Serves 8.   Cooking time: First stage: 24 hours to marinate. Second stage: 3–4 hours.   Third stage: 30 minutes

This is by far the most popular pot-roast type of dish in this family and I've tried many. It takes a little time to get ready in the first place.

4 lb (2 kg) braising beef	2 cloves garlic
3 onions	salt and pepper
1 carrot	flour
2 tomatoes or 2 tablespoons tomato purée	2 oz (50g) lard
pinch paprika	

For the Marinade

1½ pints (9 dl) water	6 peppercorns
2 tablespoons vinegar	1 bay leaf
2 slices lemon	2 cloves

For the Sauce

1–2 tablespoons sour cream	cornflour

For the Dumplings

1 egg	pinch cayenne papper
1 tablespoon water	6 oz (175 g) self-raising flour
salt	1 teaspoon melted butter
paprika	

First stage

Peel and slice the garlic. Insert the slices into the beef and tie it up neatly. Prepare the marinade by boiling together the water, vinegar, lemon, peppercorns, bay leaf and cloves. Peel and slice 1 onion. Salt and pepper the meat and put it in a bowl with the onion. Pour the boiling marinade over, cover and leave for 24 hours.

Next day, take the beef out of the marinade, dry it well and rub it with flour. Keep the marinade (see below). Peel and chop the 2 remaining onions. Scrape and chop carrot. Nick the skins of the tomatoes and plunge them in boiling water. Take out, peel and chop. Brown the meat all over in a little fat in a casserole together with the chopped onions. Add the carrot, tomatoes, paprika and 1 pint (6 dl) of the strained marinade. Cover the pot tightly and cook in a moderate oven (350°F, 180°C, Gas 4) for 3–4 hours. Listen for gentle bubbling sounds. Remove the meat when it is very tender.

Third stage

Heat the meat in the oven, when sufficiently hot take out of the pot and keep warm. Beat the egg lightly and add the water, salt, paprika and a little cayenne pepper. Add the flour and butter and blend quickly. Have the liquid in the casserole boiling on the top of the stove, drop in dumpling mixture in teaspoonfuls (give them room, they swell a lot), reduce heat, cover and simmer for 15 minutes. Take them out carefully with a slotted spoon and quickly make the sauce by straining the liquid, correcting the seasoning, thickening with cornflour and adding the sour cream. Slice the meat, surround with the dumplings covered with lots of sauce. Leftover meat can be reheated if you save some of the sauce.

A 'SOME TIME' RECIPE

Beef or Lamb Curry
Serves 6–8.   Cooking time: First stage: 2 hours for lamb, 3 hours for beef.   Second stage: 20 minutes

This is a simple curry. Buy good quality Indian or Malaysian curry powder and curry paste. Don't mix your own unless you are a curry expert (and don't read this if you are). Try to get papadams – you can get them from an Oriental delicatessen. They should be fried. If you have children who don't like curry, they can just have the side dishes; it won't hurt them to be vegetarians for a night.

1 tablespoon cooking oil
2 lb (1 kg) lean stewing beef or lamb
2 onions
1 dessertspoon curry powder (or whatever amount you like)
1 teaspoon curry paste

1 dessertspoon coconut
1 dessertspoon fruit chutney
salt
1 bay leaf
1 stock cube
cornflour to thicken

First stage

Cut up steak in 1-inch (2 cm) cubes. Peel and chop onions. Heat oil in large, heavy saucepan. Add the onions and fry gently for a few minutes. Add the meat, curry powder and paste, and brown. Keep stirring, or it will stick. Throw in the dessertspoon of coconut. Barely cover with water or stock (or just add a stock cube), add salt, chutney, bay leaf and simmer gently, covered, for 2 hours for lamb, 3 for beef. Cool, chill.

Second stage

Remove fat. Reheat. Thicken with cornflour made to a paste with a little water. Serve with boiled rice, papadams and a selection of side dishes.

Side dishes

1. Coarsely chopped tomato sprinkled with finely chopped onion
2. Salted peanuts
3. Sultanas
4. Thinly sliced bananas sprinkled with lemon juice
5. Thin slices of cucumber in plain yoghurt
6. Chopped avocado mixed with fried, chopped bacon (delicious)
7. One or two kinds of chutney

A 'NO TIME' RECIPE (PREPARED BEFOREHAND)

Veal Chops in the Oven
Serves 6: Cooking time: 1½ hours

Although veal is expensive and difficult to get, this is just about the best recipe I could give anyone, and quite elegant enough to serve at a dinner party. When you have made it once it is very quick and easy to do the initial preparation, a fact that compensates for its price and current rarity. It can then sit about waiting to go in the oven and needs no further attention. There is nothing to fry first, so you don't dirty another pan, or your kitchen.

1-inch (2 cm) thick, veal chops (I use rib chops but loin are fine too)
2 oz (50 g) melted butter
1 onion
8 oz (225 g) fresh breadcrumbs

4 oz (100 g) grated, parmesan cheese
¾ glass dry white wine
salt and pepper

Peel and finely chop the onion. Take a large shallow casserole, butter it well and sprinkle the onion over it. Salt and pepper the chops and place them in, side by side. Mix the breadcrumbs and cheese and put a little pile on each chop, pressing it down firmly. Dribble a little melted butter over the topping. Pour in the white wine and cover the casserole with the lid or foil. Put the dish in a moderately hot oven (375°F, 190°C, Gas 5) for 1½ hours. You can baste them a bit during cooking, you can watch to see that the topping does not crack and you can thicken the juice at the end for a sauce, but I never do any of those things and they always turn out beautifully. Creamed spinach is good with this dish, and I think it needs potatoes.

A 'NO TIME' RECIPE (PREPARED BEFOREHAND)

Meatballs Stroganoff
Serves 6–8. Cooking time: First stage: 45 minutes. Second stage: 30 minutes

2 lb (1 kg) finely minced meat

2 oz (50 k) butter or fat (if your mince is fatty, use less; or
   better still change your butcher)

salt and freshly milled pepper

breadcrumbs ⎫
milk ⎭ optional

For the Sauce

2 onions

4–8 oz (100–225 g) mushrooms

1 tablespoon flour

$\frac{3}{4}$ pint ($4\frac{1}{2}$ dl) stock (or water
   and a stock cube)

2 tablespoons tomato purée

1 small carton sour cream

First stage

Peel and chop the onions. Wipe and thickly slice the mushrooms. Salt and pepper the minced meat and extend it with
breadcrumbs squeezed out in milk if you like. Make into small
balls. This is very boring – there is a gadget for doing it which
makes rather large meatballs. The other gadget is one of your
children, they love rolling things into balls. The balls may only
be roundish but never mind. Brown them quickly in the butter
or fat in a frying pan, never letting them stick to the bottom.
Remove to an ovenproof pot as they brown. When they are all
done, add the mushrooms and onion to the fat remaining in the
pan, adding a bit more fat if you have to. Cook gently for a
few minutes, sprinkle with flour and stir well. Add the stock
little by little and then the tomato purée and keep stirring until
the sauce thickens. Turn down the heat, add the sour cream,
salt and pepper, and pour the sauce over the meatballs.

Second stage

Put on the lid and put into a slow oven (300°F, 150°C, Gas 2)
for 30 minutes or so. Or you can put the meatballs back into the
frying pan if it has a lid, and cook them very gently on the
top of the stove. Make sure there is plenty of sauce because
these are good served with noodles tossed around with some of
the sauce before serving. There is no need to serve a vegetable
with them.

Pork Chops Baked with Potatoes
*Serves 4.   Cooking time: First stage: 3 hours.   Second stage:
15 minutes*

A dish of delicious flavour and aroma, it has the added
advantage of the potatoes being part of the dish so there is
nothing to prepare at the end of the cooking except perhaps
another vegetable. Or just have a salad afterwards. The recipe
is taken from Elizabeth David's *French Provincial Cooking*
(Penguin £1). I have more success with large forequarter
chops than with loin myself, and though it is probably more
delicious with the fat left on them, I take the rind and edge
fat off first. It is a fairly quick dish to prepare if you have a
mandolin for slicing the potatoes thinly – a great utensil but
lethal – wear gloves.

4 pork chops	8 juniper berries
1½ lb (675 g) potatoes	parsley
small glass white wine	4 oz (100 g) ham or bacon
1 onion	2 oz (50 g) dripping
2–3 cloves garlic	salt and pepper

First stage
Peel the potatoes and slice them evenly and thinly. Peel and
slice the onion. Arrange half the potatoes and half the sliced
onion in an earthenware casserole. Near the bone of each pork
chop put a small clove of garlic and a couple of juniper berries.
Brown the chops on each side in a little dripping and put them
on top of the potatoes. Cover with the remaining potatoes and
onion, season with salt and pepper. Cover with the ham or
bacon in slices. Pour over the white wine and cover with several
layers of paper and the lid (or foil). Cook in a very slow oven
(300°F, 150°C, Gas 2) for 3 hours.

Second stage
Take off the fat and heat through. Garnish with parsley.

Australian Lamb Hot Pot

*Serves 6-8. Cooking time: First stage: 1½ hours. Second
stage: 15–20 minutes*

The advantage of this recipe is that it is relatively cheap and the
whole dinner is in one pot.

12 lamb cutlets (cut from best end of neck)	1 clove garlic
	salt
4–8 oz (100 g–225 g) each of peas, small white onions, chopped celery, chopped beans and sliced carrots	1 glass white wine
	peppercorns
	bacon fat
	bouquet garni
cornflour for thickening	

First stage

Chop garlic. Brown the cutlets in bacon fat and transfer them
to a deep casserole. Deglaze the frying pan with a little water
and add this to the casserole with the rest of the ingredients
(except for the cornflour). Cover the pot and cook in a moderate oven for about 1½ hours. Spoon some liquid over the
vegetables occasionally. When cooked the meat should slide
off the bones. Thicken the juices towards the end of cooking
with a little cornflour, mixed in some water, before putting it
in the casserole. Mashed potatoes are very good with this.

Second stage

Reheat for 15–20 minutes.

A 'NO TIME' RECIPE (LAST MINUTE)

Fillets of Fish Meunière

Serves 4. Cooking time: 10 minutes

Any flat fillets such as sole or flounder can be used.

4 fish fillets	juice of ½ lemon
2 tablespoons flour	3 oz (75 g) butter
salt	2 oz (50 g) unblanched almonds
freshly milled pepper	(optional)

Dry the fillets well and dust them with salt, pepper and flour. Melt the butter in a frying pan and when the sizzling starts to die down, put in the fish and brown them lightly on each side. It will only take a few minutes. Transfer the fish to a serving dish, pour the lemon juice into the butter remaining in the pan and pour it over the fish.

If you want to add almonds, blanch by covering them with boiling water for several minutes. Drain and take off the outer skin. Then cut the nuts into slivers. Add the nuts to the pan to brown as you turn your fish over to its second side. Boiled potatoes are good with this dish; so is creamed spinach. (page 52).

A 'NO TIME' RECIPE (LAST MINUTE)

Steak Diane

Serves 6.   Cooking time: 2 minutes per steak

6 pieces fillet steak	1 oz (25 g) butter
salt and freshly ground pepper	chopped parsley
1 clove garlic	Worcester sauce

Fillet steak. Nothing else makes a real steak Diane. I do, in fact, make a poor man's version with minute steak. It's all right, but it is not the real thing. So, fillet steak, one small slice per person, more if you can manage it. And console yourself with the fact that you can get away with half the quantity of steak you would normally need for a plain grill.

You have to cook these one at a time (two if you have a big enough pan) and each person has to start eating right away because you can't keep them. It is very very quick though so you all get to eat *some* of your dinner together.

Squeeze the garlic. Pound each steak until it is very very thin. Salt and pepper it and squeeze some garlic on each one. Melt the butter in a frying pan and when it is really hot, that is when the foaming starts to die down, put in the steak, sprinkle with chopped parsley and cook it fast, about a minute per side. Just at the end dash in a little Worcester sauce, swirl it around, and then on to a hot plate with the pan juices over. No fancy flaming with brandy or thickening the sauce please. Rinse out the pan and on with the next one. Marvellous for last-minute guests, but not more than six. Some sort of potatoes, chips are best, and a salad afterwards.

A 'NO TIME' RECIPE (LAST MINUTE)

Escalopes of Veal with Cream Sauce
Serves 6. Cooking time: 4–5 minutes each escalope

6 large, thin, escalopes
3 oz (75 g) butter
12 oz (350 g) single cream

6 tablespoons brandy or whisky
salt and pepper

This is a very quick and elegant dish.

For each large escalope (make sure you cut off the fibrous tissue around the edge or the meat will curl up) you will need $\frac{1}{2}$ oz (12 g) butter, 1 tablespoon brandy or whisky and 2 oz (50 g) cream.

Salt and pepper the meat. Melt the butter and brown the veal quickly on each side. Warm the spirit, pour over and flame, add the cream and quickly tilt the pan and keep spooning the cream over the meat as it thickens. Transfer to a warm oven while you cook the rest. The sauce is beautiful. Some plain potatoes or noodles with it, no vegetables to get mixed up with the sauce.

Actually, if you are running to veal escalopes and have just a little more time, I think it's probably better to make schnitzel (floured, egged and breadcrumbed and fried in butter and oil) as a family dinner. Take them a step further to Veal Cordon Bleu by topping the fried schnitzel with a slice of ham and a slice of mozarella cheese and into the oven until the cheese melts. A step further still, and a layer of chopped, salted, tomatoes between the ham and the cheese gives you veal Romagnola.

3. A Very Few Things To Do with Leftovers

Leftover Lamb in White Wine Sauce.   Nasi Goreng.   Miroton of Beef.   Corned Beef Hash.   Salmis of Chicken.   Fish Salad. Curry Sauce.   Savoury Pancakes.   Croquettes.

That there are a great many delicious things to do with leftovers I have no doubt (or only *some* doubts) but my skill in this direction has declined through lack of use – I hardly ever have any leftovers any more. From those far-off days when we actually had something left from a roast dinner, here are a few suggestions, one each for lamb, beef, fish and poultry.

Leftover Lamb in White Wine Sauce
Serves 4.   Cooking time: 70 minutes

8–12 oz (200–350 g) cold roast lamb
2 oz (50 g) butter
1 tablespoon flour
1 onion
1 tablespoon chopped parsley
¼ pint (1½ dl) water
¼ pint (1½ dl) white wine
2 tablespoons olive oil
salt and freshly milled pepper

Peel and chop the onion. Slice the lamb about ¼-inch (½ cm) thick. Brown the meat on each side in the butter. Add the parsley and onion and cook for 5 minutes more. Add the flour and stir in. Gradually add the water and wine, which you have mixed together, and stir until smooth. Cover and cook very gently for 1 hour. Add the oil, cook a few minutes longer, season with salt and pepper and serve with boiled rice. The lamb develops a slightly chickeny flavour and is really very good.

Nasi Goreng
Serves 4–6. Cooking time: 30 minutes. Allow time for cooking rice – see recipe

A pretty fancy way of saying leftover pork. I cook enough pork especially for this.

12 oz–1 lb (350–450 g) pork	1 teaspoon curry powder
7 oz (175 g) rice (or have it cooked already)	2 tablespoons soy sauce
1 large onion	handful raisins ⎫ optional
2 cloves garlic	handful peanuts ⎭
4 bacon rashers	2 eggs
1 hot red chilli	little butter for frying

First of all boil the rice, in the normal way. Drain and leave it to get cold. You can do this anytime before the final cooking. Chop up the pork in small pieces. Peel and coarsely chop the onion. Chop the bacon rashers. Crush the garlic. Cut the chilli in long thin strips and remove the seeds. Fry together in a little butter, the onion, garlic, bacon and pork. When brown add the curry powder and chilli. Mix in the dry, cooked rice, adding the soy sauce to get a light brown colour as the rice is heating. Add raisins and peanuts at this stage, if you like.

Beat up the 2 eggs, salt them and fry on both sides in a buttered pan, quickly like a pancake. You can serve this rolled across the top of the finished dish or cut into strips and mixed through. Serve very hot with chutney.

42 Miroton of Beef
Serves 4–6. Cooking time: 30 minutes

This is the really hard one. Boiled beef can be reheated successfully, but I must say I have never reheated roast beef without
toughening it, no matter how carefully and gently I do the
heating. I personally prefer to eat the roast beef cold, with a
sauce such as béarnaise (page 23) or marinated in sauce
ravigote (page 23). You can always serve hot potatoes with the
beef if you want it as a second dinner.

For those who want a hot dish for leftover beef other than
mincing the meat for croquettes or cottage pie, here is a beef
Miroton – a recipe from the best cook I know.

12 oz–1 lb (350–450 g) leftover roast or boiled beef
½ lb (225 g) mushrooms
3 onions
½ pint (3 dl) good beef stock (stock cubes are useful for some
   things, but they don't make good sauces)
1 tablespoon tomato purée
dash of Worcester sauce
1 oz (25 g) butter or margarine
1 tablespoon flour
salt and freshly milled pepper
1 teaspoon French mustard

Finely slice the beef. Peel and chop the onions. Wash and
finely slice the mushrooms. Melt butter in a large frying pan.
Fry onions gently until transparent. Mix in the flour and cook
for a moment before adding the stock little by little. Stir over
gentle heat until the mixture comes to the boil and is thick and
smooth. Add the beef, turning it over in the gravy. Add the
mushrooms, tomato purée, Worcester sauce, French mustard
and season with salt and freshly milled pepper. Heat the beef
very gently. Serve with baked potatoes and salad.

*Serves 4–6.   Cooking   time: 15–20   minutes.   Allow   several
hours in refrigerator*

1 lb (450 g) potatoes   nut of butter
1 lb (450 g) corned beef   salt and freshly milled pepper
4 tablespoons fat (butter or
    margarine)

Finely chop or mince the corned beef. Peel the potatoes, boil
them, then drain and mash thoroughly with a nut of butter and
season well with salt and pepper (it should be dryish). Mix
together the corned beef and mashed potato. Pat it down firmly
in a bowl, cover and refrigerate for several hours.

Take a large frying pan and melt 2 tablespoons of fat, butter
or margarine in it. When it is quite hot, put in a layer of the
hash, about $\frac{1}{2}$ inch (1 cm) thick and firmly packed. Cook over
moderate heat until it is brown and crusty underneath. Reverse
on to a large plate, put the other 2 tablespoons of butter in the
pan and slide the hash back in to brown the other side. Serve
with fried eggs on top.

Salmis of Chicken
Serves 3–4.   Cooking time: 10–15 minutes

4 shallots   salt and freshly milled pepper
8 oz (225 g) chopped or   pinch thyme
    minced chicken   pinch rosemary
small glass sherry   1 tablespoon lemon juice
4 oz (100 g) chopped olives   2 tablespoons butter
$\frac{1}{2}$ pint (3 dl) chicken stock or
    gravy

Peel and chop shallots. Fry them gently in the butter. Add the
rest of the ingredients and simmer for 5 minutes. Serve with
rice.

You can also serve leftover chicken, chopped up, in a chicken
velouté (see page 19) with some tarragon or sautéd mushrooms.
Chicken in a sauce is also good in pancakes or as a filling for
vol-au-vent cases.

Serves 4–6. Time taken: 20 minutes. Allow 20 minutes for making aïoli

This seems too beautiful a dish to use just for leftover fish, but I include it here in case you bake a large fish and prefer a cold dish to use it up.

1 lb (450 g) cooked fish (it can be half smoked and half fresh if you wish)	1 tablespoon capers
	2–3 hardboiled eggs
	parsley to garnish
½ pint (3 dl) aïoli (see page 21)	juice of lemon
2 heads fennel or ½ cucumber	cayenne pepper

Flake the fish with a fork. Finely slice the fennel, keeping the leaves to garnish. If using cucumber, peel, finely slice it, salt and drain well. Mix fish, fennel or cucumber and capers with ¾ of the aïoli and flavour with the lemon juice and cayenne to taste. Pile on a dish, cover with the remaining aïoli, sprinkle with chopped parsley or the chopped fennel leaves and garnish with slices of hardboiled egg.

Curry Sauce

Makes ¾ pint (scant ½ litre). Cooling time: 55–65 minutes

I use this sauce for curried sausages, of which my family is extremely fond. I cook the sausages first, drain them, and then leave them in the sauce to absorb the flavour before reheating.

½–¾ pint (3–4½ dl) of chicken stock (or cubes)	1 tablespoon good curry powder
small glass of white wine	½ teaspoon ground ginger
4 oz (100 g) desiccated coconut	½ tablespoon salt
2 tablespoons oil	6 peppercorns
2 onions	2 bay leaves
4 sticks celery	juice of ½ lemon
3 tomatoes	1 tablespoon redcurrant jelly
	1 dessertspoon cornflour

Boil stock and pour over coconut. Leave for 15 minutes. Strain. Peel and chop the onions. Nick the skins of the tomatoes, plunge them in boiling water, drain, then peel and chop. Chop

the celery. Fry the onions and celery in the oil, over a gentle
heat, until they are soft. Add the tomatoes and fry a little
longer then add all the herbs and spices. Pour on the stock and
wine, and simmer, covered, for 45 minutes. Sieve the sauce, then
add the lemon juice, redcurrant jelly, and thicken with cornflour, mixed with a little cold water. You can always leave all
the vegetables in, remembering, however, to remove the bay
leaves.

There are several ways in which my children will eat practically anything – cooked in individual dishes, cooked on
skewers, wrapped up in pancakes or made into croquettes.
These last two are valuable to keep in mind when using up
leftovers. They also make light supper or lunch dishes.

Savoury Pancakes
Makes 19–20 pancakes. Cooking pancakes: 35–40 minutes.
Cooking filling: 35–40 minutes

This recipe is similar to the pancake recipe for cannelloni,
but with a slight variation.

8 oz (225 g) sifted plain flour
4 eggs
½ teaspoon salt

¾ pint (4½ dl) milk (or ½ milk
½ water)
2 tablespoons melted butter
little oil for frying

You can mix this all in a blender or sift flour and salt into a
bowl, and beat eggs into the flour, one at a time. Gradually
beat in the liquid, then the butter. Strain. The mixture should
stand for an hour or two in order to improve the batter.
Oil the pan and heat until smoking; you will have to adjust
the heat for the first few. The pan shouldn't need any more
oil once you've cooked one or two. They should take a minute
or less to brown on each side. Start off with about 1½ tablespoons of mixture per pancake, tilt the pan quickly to cover
the bottom. Try and make them fairly thin. When one side
is browned, loosen with a spatula and turn with your fingers
or toss. Pile them up as you go, putting a piece of foil between every 4 or 5. If not wanted immediately, refrigerate or
freeze them, in which case put in a polythene bag and tie
tightly. If refrigerated, eat within 5 days.

When you come to fill the pancakes, chop up the meat, chicken, fish or vegetables you are using into small pieces and bind with a sauce. Use a béchamel (page 19), or a velouté (page 19) if you have some stock, and season well. The filling should be fairly solid so use a thick sauce. Save a little for later. Roll up the filling in the pancakes, place them in a buttered ovenproof dish and spread the remaining sauce over the top. You could thin it down first with a little cream. Heat in a moderate oven (350°F, 180°C, Gas 4) for 30 minutes. Serve for a family meal, a lunch dish or a dinner party first course.

Croquettes

Serves 4–6.   Cooking time: 1 hour.   In addition allow 1½ hours for cooling

1 lb (450 g) cooked meat, poultry or fish

herbs (appropriate to the meat or fish you are using)

2 oz (50 g) butter

2 oz (50 g) flour

salt and pepper

2 eggs

breadcrumbs

oil for frying

For the Sauce

½ pint (3 dl) milk or ¼ pint (1½ dl) milk

¼ pint (1½ dl) appropriate stock

1 oz (25 g) flour

salt and pepper

1 oz (25 g) butter

Mince the cooked meat or poultry or flake the fish. Mix into a very thick white sauce (see page 18) or sauce made partly with milk and partly with the appropriate stock. Cook, uncovered, until the mixture is really solid. Season very well, using whatever herbs you like, with the meat or fish you are using. Leave until quite cold. Form into ovals. Lightly beat the eggs. Now comes the main thing to remember: dust the croquettes with flour and then dip them, first in the egg and then in the breadcrumbs. Do this *twice* so that they are well sealed. You will then get a crisp outside and a good creamy interior. If possible, leave them for a while in the refrigerator after coating, before frying. Deep fry in very hot oil for 5 minutes. A fresh tomato sauce (page 68) is good with meat croquettes, so is a cream sauce (page 20).

4. Vegetables

Gratin Dauphinois. Johannsen's Temptation. Potatoes Anna. Roësti. Braised Leeks or Celery. Mushrooms in the Pan. Peas with Onion and Lettuce. Cabbage with Green Pepper and Onion. Fried Cabbage. Creamed Spinach. Spinach in Fila (or Phyllo) Pastry. Courgettes with Fresh Herbs. Courgettes with Tomatoes.

If your children groan and fall about, as mine do, at the mere mention of most vegetables, the last thing you want is a lot of new vegetable recipes. I try not to worry too much about their vegetable intake; I've never met an adult who didn't like vegetables, so Nature must take care of it for us eventually. My children, however, will eat almost any vegetable raw, so a dish of raw vegetables, with a mayonnaise dip, often solves this problem.

My own preference with most vegetables is to boil them for as short a time as possible and serve them with a lump of butter. Never leave cooked vegetables in their cooking water. If they have to wait a bit take them off the heat and drain them well before they are fully cooked. Then put them back in their saucepans (if you haven't an oven on) with a good lump of butter, toss them in the butter, cover, and put over the lowest possible heat to finish cooking very slowly in the butter and steam. This applies particularly to small new potatoes, carrots and whole beans.

The idea that people are becoming so used to frozen vegetables that fresh ones taste 'unreal', is shocking, and should send us all rushing out to dig up a bit of earth to plant something straight away. Lots of vegetables are easy to grow and can be grown in any odd container on a window ledge, or on a back step.

The first recipes are for potatoes. They are such delicious *and* nutritious vegetables it is a pity more trouble is not taken in their preparation. And weight for weight potatoes contain $2\frac{1}{2}$ times less carbohydrate than bread. The first three recipes are particularly useful as they cook gently for quite a long time in the oven, needing no last-minute attention. They all use finely sliced potatoes, of the waxy variety, rather than floury. This operation is quick and easy if you have a mandolin – a great but lethal gadget – wear gloves.

For salads see the 'weekend food' chapter.

Gratin Dauphinois
Serves 4–6. Cooking time: $1\frac{1}{2}$ hours

2 lb (1 kg) waxy potatoes   1 pint cream
1 clove garlic
salt and freshly milled pepper

Peel and finely slice the potatoes. Soak in cold water for 15 minutes. Drain and shake them dry in a teatowel. Butter an ovenproof dish and rub it with garlic. Layer the potatoes, seasoning them with salt and pepper and pour over the cream. Bake in a slow oven (300°F, 150°C, Gas 2) for $1\frac{1}{2}$ hours. So delicious it can be eaten on its own. This dish can also be made with the addition of a thin layer of grated cheese between the layers of potato, and milk with an egg beaten into it, instead of cream.

Serves 4–6.   Cooking time: 1½–2 hours

2 lb (1 kg) waxy potatoes
2 large onions
1 tin anchovies
½ pint (3 dl) cream (sour is
  preferable)

¼ pint (1½ dl) milk
1 oz (25 g) butter or margarine
freshly ground pepper

Peel and finely slice the potatoes, or cut them into straws. Peel
and finely chop the onions. Melt the butter and cook the onions
gently in a covered pan until they are soft. Butter a casserole
and layer the potatoes, onions and anchovies, finishing up with
a layer of potatoes. Season with pepper. Do not add salt as the
anchovies are salty enough. Warm the sour cream and milk,
pour over, bring to boil on top of the stove with the lid on.
Cook in a low to moderate oven (300°F, 150°C, Gas 2 or
350°F, 180°C, Gas 4) for 1½ hours with the lid off. If your
oven dish can't start off on top of the stove, increase the time
in the oven to 2 hours.

Potatoes Anna
Serves 4–6.   Cooking time: 45–50 minutes

2 lb (1 kg) waxy potatoes
salt and freshly milled pepper

3 oz (75 g) butter or margarine
parsley (to garnish)

Peel and finely slice the potatoes. Soak in cold water for 15
minutes then dry well. Season them with salt and pepper.
Butter an ovenproof dish and fill it with overlapping layers of
potato slices, spreading butter between the layers and on the
top. Bake in a very hot oven (425°F, 220°C, Gas 7) for 45
minutes. Loosen the edges and turn it out on to a round plate.
It should be brown and crisp. Surround with parsley or whole
mushrooms.

50　Roesti

Serves 4–6.　Cooking time: 30 minutes

A sort of Swiss potato pancake, very popular with my children.

2 lb (1 kg) waxy potatoes
butter or margarine to fry
salt and freshly milled pepper

Grate raw potatoes, soak in cold water for 15 minutes, drain and dry very well by rolling up in teatowels or paper towelling. Take a heavy frying pan with a lid and melt enough butter or margarine to cover the bottom well. Put in the grated potato, about $\frac{1}{2}$ inch (1 cm) thick, pressing it down firmly. Salt and pepper. Cover the pan and cook over moderate heat for about 15 minutes. Lift the edge of the potatoes with a spatula and if the under side is golden and crunchy, turn it over to brown the other side, adding some more butter. If your pan is large, reverse the roësti on to a plate and then slide it back in. I leave the lid off to brown the second side. You can add other things, such as grated onion, but potatoes cooked in this simple way have an interesting flavour and texture on their own. The Swiss often serve this with creamy veal dishes but it's also good with plain grilled or fried meats.

Braised Leeks or Celery
Serves 4.　Cooking time: 15 minutes

1 lb (450 g) leeks
1 stock cube

salt and freshly milled pepper
nut of butter

Use small leeks if you can get them, or cut off the green tops and slice the white part in half lengthwise. Be sure to wash them very well. Boil in plenty of salted water until half cooked. Drain, and add a nut of butter and a little stock, not enough to cover the leeks. Boil gently with the lid off until the leeks are cooked and the stock and butter are reduced to a little syrupy sauce.

　　Celery can be cooked in the same way. Cut into lengths, so that it fits in the pan.

Mushrooms in the Pan

Serves 6–8.   Cooking time: 30 minutes

1 lb (450 g) field mushrooms	butter
salt and freshly milled pepper	little milk

Just an easy way to cook mushrooms if you have a number of other dishes to attend to. Use the field kind if possible. Wash mushrooms, or wipe them over, and take off the stalks. Season with salt and pepper and place a lump of butter on each. Put them in an ovenproof dish in one layer with a little milk at the bottom. Cover with the lid or foil and cook in a moderate oven (350°F, 180°C, Gas 4) for 30 minutes.

Peas with Onion and Lettuce

Serves 6–8.   Cooking time: 35 minutes

1 lb (450 g) shelled peas	salt and freshly milled pepper
4 small onions or 2 medium ones	sprig of thyme or sprinkling of dried thyme
1 lettuce heart	4 rashers bacon or 2 slices ham (if you have it, but neither is essential)
nut of butter	

Pod peas, if using fresh. Peel onions, if using medium ones, quarter them. Wash lettuce and shred or quarter it. Chop the bacon or ham into small pieces. Put everything together (no water) in a heavy saucepan without a lid. Start off over medium heat (shaking the pan) for about 5 minutes, then cover and cook over low heat for 30 minutes, shaking the pan from time to time. This dish is cooked in the steam given off by the vegetables. There may be a little juice left at the end. You can thicken this a bit if you like, or reduce it by boiling it fast with the lid off before serving the peas.

Cabbage with Green Pepper and Onion
Serves 6–8. Cooking time: 45 minutes

1 large white cabbage   1 green pepper
1 tablespoon olive oil   salt and freshly ground pepper
1 onion

Shred cabbage and wash but do not dry. Peel and slice the onion. Slice and de-seed the green pepper. Put olive oil in a saucepan, together with the onion, green pepper and cabbage (no extra water). Season with salt and lots of black pepper and cover. Cook over moderately low heat for about 45 minutes. Stir occasionally in order to distribute the onion and green pepper through the cabbage.

Fried Cabbage
Serves 4–6. Cooking time: 10 minutes

1 large cabbage
butter, margarine or olive oil for frying
tomato purée (optional)

Shred, wash and dry cabbage. Fry, uncovered, in a large pan, in butter, margarine, a mixture of butter and oil, or olive oil only, over moderately high heat. Don't let the cabbage get limp, but it doesn't matter if a few bits brown. You need to stir it nearly all the time but it doesn't take long. If you happen to have some tomato purée, try adding that. When the cabbage is nearly cooked, pour in some tomato purée and let it reduce down as the cabbage finishes cooking.

Creamed Spinach
Serves 4–6. Cooking time: 30 minutes

2 lb (1 kg) fresh spinach or 2 (12 oz) (350 g) packets frozen
  spinach
1 onion
1 oz (25 g) butter

1 teaspoon cornflour ⎫
1 cup milk ⎬ or ½ pint (3 dl) cream
⎭
pinch nutmeg
salt and freshly ground pepper

Wash spinach well. Do not drain. Place in a large saucepan and let it cook in the water clinging to the leaves. Cover with a lid and boil for 15–20 minutes. Drain well and chop finely. Peel and finely chop the onion and fry in butter until soft. Add the spinach. Add the cream and mix through until thoroughly heated. If using cornflour, mix it with the milk and add to the spinach mixture. Stir until it comes to the boil. Season with nutmeg, salt and pepper.

Spinach in Fila (or Phyllo) Pastry
Serves 6–8.   Cooking time: 30–45 minutes

1 pkt fila (phyllo) pastry   chopped spinach
feta cheese   melted butter
pinch nutmeg

Included at the request of my non-spinach eaters, but they will eat anything wrapped in fila (phyllo) pastry.

Take well drained and well chopped spinach (and frozen is useful here, if you get rid of all the moisture) and mix it with some crumbled feta cheese and a little nutmeg. Cut the pastry into long strips 3 or 4 inches (7 to 10 cms) wide and brush with melted butter. Put a spoonful of filling near the end and fold the end of the pastry over it crosswise to make a triangle. Then fold over again and again until the whole strip is folded into a triangle. Brush with melted butter. Repeat with the rest of the pastry and place the little pies on an oiled tray. Bake in a moderately hot oven (375°F, 190°C, Gas 5) for 30–45 minutes, or until crisp and golden.

The following two recipes are Elizabeth David's, taken from her *French Provincial Cooking* (Penguin £1), very simple and good.

Courgettes with Fresh Herbs
Serves 4–6.   Cooking time: 15 minutes

1 lb (450 g) courgettes
1 oz (50 g) butter
lemon juice

1 tablespoon finely chopped
   parsley/chervil/chives
salt and pepper

Wash the courgettes and cut into thin bias-cut rounds, salt and leave to drain for an hour or so. Rinse off salt and put them in a saucepan containing a very little boiling water. Cook for 10 minutes. Drain and finish cooking by frying gently in butter, turning them over and adding a tablespoon of finely chopped parsley, chervil or chives. Season with salt and pepper and a squeeze of lemon jucie.

Courgettes with Tomatoes
Serves 4–6.   Cooking time: 20 minutes

1 lb (450 g) courgettes
8 oz (225 g) tomatoes
2 tablespoons olive oil

1 clove garlic
salt, pepper

Wash and slice the courgettes. Sprinkle with salt and leave to drain for an hour or so. Rinse off salt and dry. Chop or press the garlic. Nick the skins of the tomatoes and plunge them in boiling water. Peel and chop. Gently fry the courgettes in the olive oil, with the garlic, turning them over so that they do not stick. Add the tomatoes and continue cooking until the tomatoes have softened and turned almost to a sauce. Season with salt and freshly ground pepper. Good hot or cold.

5. Weekend Food

Kipper Pâtè. Chicken Liver Pâtè. Cold Dishes: Chicken Salad. Vitello Tonnato (Veal with Tuna Sauce). Salade Niçoise. Pork and Veal Terrine. Salmon Mousse. Salads: Cold Potato Salad. Hot Potato Salad. Bean Salad. Cucumber Salad. Villa d'Este Aubergine. Ratatouille. Coleslaw. Tomato Salad. Hot Dishes: Cannelloni. Quiche Lorraine. Onion or Leek Tart. Kedgeree. Meat Sauce for Spaghetti. Spaghetti di Mare. Puffed Potatoes. Marinade for Steak. Marinade for Lamb Chops or Kebabs. Marinade for Pork Chops. Marinade for Barbecued Chicken.

I know it is unrealistic to expect to have a weekend with everyone at home, relaxed, unhurried, and wanting to eat at the same time. Sometimes it does happen however, and a long, lazy weekend meal can be one of the very good things of family life. Small things can make it seem more of an occasion, a pretty tablecloth, using china you usually keep for guests, taking the whole meal outside if it's possible for you. Because I find weekend eating and drinking particularly enjoyable, I always intend to do a good deal of organization and preparation beforehand so that I can produce delicious meals with seemingly effortless ease. Here's a list of things I aim to do. I actually manage to do some of them some of the time.

1. Decide on Friday (Thursday would be better still) exactly what to have for each weekend meal. That is, decide on two breakfasts and four other meals which can be moved around according to circumstances. These four meals must be flexible; it does not matter whether the main meal is to be at lunchtime or in the evening.

2. If possible, do all the advance cooking and preparation on Friday, or Thursday or Friday night if working. All the cold dishes I have listed later can be prepared ahead, and the hot dishes either fully or partly prepared. Make sure there is cake or biscuits or something which will do for pudding or afternoon tea if necessary. Certainly one meal should be *completely* prepared. Cannelloni may take ages to prepare, but it's worth it when you get home late and have nothing to do but put it in the oven, set the table and it's ready.

3. Have one small delicious thing on hand in case friends come in unexpectedly. I suppose there's nothing against giving it to them if you *are* expecting them. There is a chicken liver and kipper pâté in this chapter and a tuna one on page 87. They also make a good easy first course, with hot toast, at a dinner party.

4. Have one meal planned which can be easily stretched to include extra guests without anyone getting flustered. This can be done without being wasteful – salad meals consisting of three or four different dishes always go around a few more if you have extra hot bread; a spaghetti sauce will cover just as much spaghetti as you decide, at the last minute, to cook; a salade niçoise is easily stretched by adding another tin of tuna (which otherwise stays in your pantry) and some extra lettuce (which you would have in any case). I have included four marinades for different types of meat. These are useful for barbecues in the summer – a perfect way for both feeding and entertaining your family – but can just as well be used for main meals in any season. Marinating meat is a good way of tenderizing the cheaper cuts and adds a delicious flavour.

Serves 4.   Cooking time: 20 minutes.   Allow time to chill

8 oz (125 g) kipper fillets
juice of ½ lemon
8 oz (75 g) softened, unsalted
  butter

freshly ground black pepper
mace (nutmeg will do)
1 tablespoon single cream

Dot the kipper fillets with butter, cover with foil and bake for 20 minutes at (350°F, 180°C, Gas 4). Cool. Put them through a sieve or food mill or blend in an electric blender. Add the rest of the ingredients, pack it into a pot and chill.

  If you want to avoid the smell, buy canned kippers and heat them in the can, or buy the frozen kind and heat them in boiling water in their bags. Then put everything into an electric blender and blend until smooth.

Chicken Liver Pâté

Serves 6.   Cooking time: 20 minutes

8 oz (225 g) chicken livers
4 oz (100 g) butter
1 small onion, finely minced
1 teaspoon salt

1 teaspoon dry mustard
cayenne pepper
¼ teaspoon ground nutmeg
⅛ teaspoon ground cloves

Cover the chicken livers with water and simmer for 20 minutes. Put them through the mincer, add all the rest of the ingredients, then pound them together well. Or the mincing and mixing can all be done in a blender.

COLD DISHES

Chicken Salad

Serves 6.   Cooking time: for chicken: 45–60 minutes

I always boil roasting chickens, it's much better than roasting them for eating cold. Do them the same way as for chicken pie (page 28) and keep the stock.

1 (3½ lb) (1¾ kg) chicken
2 hardboiled eggs
1 heaped teaspoon finely chopped or grated onion
1 tablespoon finely chopped celery or fennel
1 dessertspoon chopped parsley
¼ pint (1½ dl) mayonnaise (made with a little mustard)
salt and pepper

Take the meat off the bones and cut into large bite-sized pieces. Thin down the mayonnaise slightly with boiling water. You will need a lot. (Every time I try to economize on the amount of mayonnaise in any dish, the result is always disappointing.) Chop the hardboiled eggs. Put everything in a bowl and mix well.

Vitello Tonnato (Veal with Tuna Sauce)

Serves 10–12.   Cooking time: 2½ hours.   Allow extra time to chill.

This is expensive to make as an everyday family dish, but it is a very elegant main lunch dish and goes a long way. In this recipe the veal is browned and then covered for the rest of the cooking, a much better way of treating veal than roasting in an open pan.

4 lb (2 kg) boneless rolled leg of veal
parsley, pinch thyme, 2 bay leaves, salt and pepper
1 large onion
½ pint (3 dl) mayonnaise (page 20)
2 carrots
2 celery stalks
lemon juice to taste
2 cloves garlic
olive oil for browning
1 tin tuna
capers
1 tin anchovies
parsley } to garnish
1 cup dry white wine
lemon slices

Peel and chop onion. Scrape and slice carrots. Wash and chop celery. Crush garlic. Brown the veal in olive oil in a fireproof pot. Add the onion, carrots, celery, garlic, tuna, anchovies, white wine and seasonings and bring to the boil. Cover and simmer slowly for 2 hours in a slow oven (325°F, 170°C, Gas 3).

Remove meat and leave to chill. Put the contents of pot into a saucepan without a lid. Bring to the boil and reduce by half. Purée or sieve. (I use the blender.) Chill, and then blend with the mayonnaise and lemon juice to taste.

Slice the veal thinly and serve, either with some of the sauce spread between the slices, or with the sauce served separately. I like the sauce between the slices and left overnight. In either case, it is good served on a bed of cold fluffy rice, garnished with capers, parsley and lemon. You could serve a green salad either with it or afterwards, nothing more.

Salade Niçoise
Serves (see recipe).   Time taken: 40 minutes

And before anyone tells me this is not the authentic recipe, let me say I have never eaten two the same, around Nice or any-where else. I will list the ingredients I use; you decide on the proportions according to how many people you are making it for, which ingredients you like best, and what you have on hand.

1 tin tuna	black olives
lettuce	garlic
red or green peppers	parsley
onion	French dressing (see page 22)
potatoes (the waxy kind)	hardboiled eggs and anchovies
celery	to garnish
tomatoes	salt and freshly milled pepper

Flake the tuna, leaving the pieces fairly large. Wash lettuce and tear into pieces. Slice and de-seed the red or green peppers. Peel onion and break into thin rings. Boil the potatoes; don't overcook them, they should be quite firm. Wash and slice the celery. Cut the tomatoes into wedges. Crush the garlic. Chop the parsley. Put all the ingredients into a large bowl. Toss the salad in French dressing and garnish with hardboiled egg quarters and anchovy fillets. Serve with hot crusty bread and butter, or black bread.

60 Pork and Veal Terrine

Serves 4–6.   Cooking time: 2½ hours.   Allow time to cool

If your butcher sells ready-minced pork and veal, use this. It is usually very fatty but you need a high proportion of fat for a terrine.

2 lb (1 kg) mixed veal and pork	¼ pint (1½ dl) white wine
8 oz (225 g) ham (optional)	1 tablespoon brandy (optional)
5 juniper berries	¼ lb (100 g) bacon
6 peppercorns	2 bay leaves
1 clove garlic	salt and pepper
pinch thyme and marjoram	

Dice the ham. Crush peppercorns, juniper berries and garlic. Cut bacon in small strips. Mix everything together, except the bacon and bay leaves, in a large bowl and let it stand for 2 hours. If you want to be sure of your seasoning, fry a spoonful to try. This is a nuisance but better than being disappointed in a dish which depends so much on its seasoning.

Line a terrine or ovenproof container with a lid with half the little strips of bacon. Pack the mixture in (it should fill the terrine) cover with the other half of the bacon strips and press the bay leaves on top. Cover. Place the terrine in a tin of water and cook in a slow oven (300°F, 150°C, Gas 2) for 2½ hours. Cool. Serve in slices from the terrine unless everyone makes a fuss about the fat and jelly which will have set around it, in which case, remove it from the container and scrape all that off before slicing.

I like it with potato salad, a tossed green salad and crusty bread.

Salmon Mousse

Serves 6–8.   Time taken: 20 minutes.   Allow several hours to chill

1 lb (450 g) cooked or tinned salmon	¼ pint (1½ dl) double cream
½ pint (3 dl) fish stock or water in which you have dissolved	2 egg whites
	lemon juice, salt, cayenne pepper
1 tablespoon of powdered gelatine	

Mash the salmon well and add the ½ pint of stock. Or combine 61
them in the blender. Season well with salt, cayenne pepper and
a squeeze of lemon juice, and chill until almost set. Beat the
cream and fold it in. Last of all fold in the stiffly beaten egg
whites. Turn into a lightly oiled mould (it turns out easily
or a soufflé dish if you can't face the unmoulding. Chill.
Lovely with cucumber salad.

You can use the same recipe with leftover chicken, in which
case you need some good chicken stock and other herbs so
that it will not be dull. You should mince the chicken if you
haven't got a blender. Ham mousse can be made in the same
way (again, mince the ham if you haven't got a blender). Add
a little tomato purée and parsley. For crab mousse add a small
amount of chives and mustard, and 2 oz (50 g) mayonnaise to
the mixture.

SALADS

Cold Potato Salad
Serves 4–6.   Time taken: 20 minutes

2 lb (1 kg) waxy new potatoes   1 tablespoon chopped parsley
1 tablespoon olive oil   1 tablespoon chopped celery
scant ½ pint (3 dl) mayon-   2 hardboiled eggs
   naise (page 20)   salt and freshly milled pepper
1 tablespoon grated onion

Boil the potatoes in their skins until only just cooked. Do *not*
overcook. Drain and leave until cold enough to handle. Cut up.
Pour the olive oil over them as you put them into the bowl.
Thin down the mayonnaise with some boiling water. Fold it
gently through the potatoes, seasoning with the onion, parsley,
celery, chopped hardboiled eggs, and salt and pepper.

Hot Potato Salad
Serves 4–6.   Cooking time: 20 minutes

2 lb (1 kg) waxy new potatoes   1 tablespoon chopped parsley
5 or 6 rashers of bacon   1 tablespoon chopped chives
¼ pint (1½ dl) French dressing   salt and pepper
1 tablespoon grated onion

Boil the potatoes in their skins. Do not overcook. Chop the bacon and fry until crisp. Slice the potatoes as soon as you can handle them and put them in a bowl. Mix in the bacon, fat as well. Toss gently. Pour over the French dressing, add the onion, parsley and chives if you have any and season with salt and pepper. Toss again gently.

Good for lunch with frankfurters and sliced tomatoes.

Bean Salad
Time taken: 10 minutes

tinned beans (lima, kidney, butter beans' whatever combination you like)
grated onion
French dressing (page 22)
chopped parsley

It is important to drain, rinse and dry the beans. Toss them with French dressing and season with the onion and lots of chopped parsley. Chill.

Cucumber Salad
Serves 4.   Time taken: 10 minutes.   Allow time for cucumber to drain and chill

1 large cucumber
$\frac{1}{4}$ pint ($1\frac{1}{2}$ dl) sour cream
1 tablespoon vinegar
salt

$\frac{1}{2}$ tablespoon finely chopped onion
$\frac{1}{2}$ tablespoon finely chopped green pepper

Peel and slice cucumber, salt and leave to drain, this stops you getting a watery salad. Add a good tablespoon of vinegar to the cream and fold it through the cucumbers, adding the finely chopped onion and pepper. Chill.

Another way is to soak the cucumber slices in vinegar for several hours, drain well and just cover with fresh cream.

Serves 6.   Cooking time: 15 minutes.   Allow time to chill

3 medium aubergines
little oil for frying
1 clove garlic
2 tomatoes
pinch oregano

pinch thyme
1 teaspoon vinegar
1 teaspoon sugar
3 tablespoons stock
salt and pepper

This is my favourite way with aubergines, and comes via a friend from the beautiful Villa d'Este on Lake Como so it *must* be good.

Slice aubergines about $\frac{1}{4}$ in ($\frac{1}{2}$ cm) thick. Sprinkle with salt and leave for 10–15 minutes to extract the moisture. Rinse, drain and dry. (Do both sides.) Fry slices in oil. Remove and salt and pepper them. Crush garlic. Skin and slice tomatoes. Add the garlic to the pan together with the tomatoes, oregano, thyme, vinegar, stock and sugar. Cook for a few minutes, not long enough to reduce the tomatoes to a pulp. Put the aubergines back in and continue cooking for a short time. Transfer to a glass bowl and cool (not chill). This is rather oily unless you have drained the aubergines very well, but you can pour off some oil after it has cooled. I like this by itself, with some crackers or a roll, but it's good with cold meat or a barbecue too.

Ratatouille
Serves 8.   Cooking time: 70 minutes.   Allow 1 hour for salting of aubergines

Elizabeth David's recipe, taken from *French Provincial Cooking* (Penguin £1), for ratatouille is the best one I've ever made, so here it is. It can be eaten hot or cold and reheats well. Do not overcook the vegetables, mushy ratatouille loses its character. The amounts can be varied; I do not use as much red pepper and usually only one aubergine weighing about a pound.

3 medium-sized onions
3 large aubergines
3 courgettes
3 sweet red peppers
4 large tomatoes

2 cloves garlic
coriander seeds
pinch basil or parsley
1–2 coffee-cups olive oil
salt and pepper

Peel and thinly slice the onions. Dice the aubergines and courgettes, sprinkle with salt and put in a colander with a plate and
a weight on top. Leave for 1 hour to enable the moisture to be
drawn out. De-seed and slice red peppers. Peel and chop
tomatoes. Chop garlic and crush coriander seeds. After 1 hour
rinse, drain and dry the aubergines.

Heat olive oil in a large frying pan. Put in the onions and
when they are soft add aubergines, courgettes, peppers and
garlic. Cover and cook gently for 40 minutes. Add tomatoes
and coriander and season with salt and pepper. Cover and
cook for another 30 minutes. Serve sprinkled with basil or
chopped parsley.

Coleslaw

Serves 6.   Time taken: 20 minutes.   Allow time to chill

Another good weekend salad because it goes well with cold or
hot meats or barbecues. I don't think it hurts to be kept a day
or so. Lots of children who wouldn't eat cooked cabbage if
they were starving love it if it's raw.

$\frac{1}{2}$ white cabbage heart
1 tablespoon grated onion
1 tablespoon grated carrot
1 tablespoon chopped gherkins

2 teaspoons capers
$\frac{1}{4}$ pint (1$\frac{1}{2}$ dl) thinned-down
mayonnaise (only thinned
down so it doesn't sit in a
solid lump)

Finely slice cabbage leaves. Wash, drain and dry well (just roll
up in tea towels). Add the onion, carrot, gherkins and capers
and toss well with the mayonnaise. Chill. Toss again, just
before serving.

Time taken: 10 minutes

tomatoes   salt and pepper
French dressing (page 22)   chopped basil

Tomatoes should only be in a salad by themselves (I *know* I
put them in the niçoise). Cut them in thick slices and toss them,
in French dressing at the last minute. Season with salt and
pepper and lots of chopped basil in the summer. Tomatoes are
nicer if you take them out of the refrigerator some time before
you need to eat them.

HOT DISHES

Cannelloni

*Makes 19–20 Cannelloni.   Cooking time: batter: 15 minutes,
plus 1 hour to stand.   Filling: 45 minutes.   Sauces: 30 minutes.
Final Cooking: 30 minutes*

This takes rather a long time to make so do it in stages while
you are doing other things. Cannelloni are pancakes filled with
meat, and covered with two sauces (one tomato and one white
sauce), and topped with grated cheese. The dish can be
completely prepared, covered with polythene and left in the
refrigerator. Heat up in a moderate oven for about 30 minutes.
Children are usually very fond of them.

The Pancakes

8 oz (225 g) plain flour   2 tablespoons oil
salt   1 pint (6 dl) milk
2 eggs $\frac{1}{2}$ oz (12$\frac{1}{2}$ g) butter

The Filling

2 lb (1 kg) finely minced steak   1 teaspoon dried oregano
1 large onion   salt and pepper
1 clove garlic   4 oz (100 g) butter or margarine
1 dessertspoon tomato paste   2 tablespoons flour
1 bay leaf

T.F.C.—C

White Sauce

1 tablespoon butter or margarine	½ pint (3 dl) milk
1 tablespoon flour	salt and pepper
	pinch nutmeg

Tomato Sauce

½ lb (225 g) tomatoes	oil for frying
1 clove garlic	salt and pepper
1 tablespoon chopped onion	1 bay leaf

To Garnish

3 oz (75 g) grated Cheddar cheese	2 oz (50 g) grated Parmesan

To Make the Pancakes

Sift flour and salt. Make a well in the centre and put in eggs and oil. Using a wooden spoon, gradually stir in the flour, mixing from the centre. Add the milk gradually and mix to a smooth batter. Let it stand for 1 hour. Butter a frying pan and heat until it smokes. Pour in about 2 tablespoons of the mixture. Brown on one side, turn it over with a spatula and fingers, or toss. Brown the other side. Throw it out. The first one always goes peculiar. The next 19 will be beautiful. Rotate the pan to spread the mixture thinly.

To Make the Filling

Peel and finely chop onion. Crush garlic. Melt the butter and fry the mince with the onion, until the onion is soft and the meat browned. Add the other ingredients, except the flour, cover, and cook slowly for 30 minutes. Stir in the flour. Keep cooking it slowly, stirring occasionally, for another 15 minutes (just to cook the flour).

To Make the Sauces

White Sauce

(See page 18)

Gently fry the tomatoes with the crushed clove of garlic, onion and bay leaf in the oil until they are quite soft. Season with pepper and salt. Purée.

To Assemble the Cannelloni

Butter a long, shallow, ovenproof dish. Spoon the filling into the pancakes and roll up. Put them close together down the dish. Cover with wide lengthwise stripes of the two sauces. Grate cheese liberally over the top, adding some grated Parmesan as well. Reheat in a moderate oven for 30 minutes.

Quiche Lorraine
Serves 6. Cooking time: 1 hour

These open tarts make lovely weekend dishes for lunch or supper and can be partly prepared beforehand if you want to. They are easy to make if you use a good frozen puff pastry. I don't say reputations are made in this way, but after all, this is family cooking. If you want to make your own pastry, and there is no doubt it will be a much better tart, particularly the vegetable ones, this is an easy one.

The Pastry

6 oz (150 g) plain flour	3 tablespoons iced water
3 oz (75 g) butter or margarine	pinch salt

The Filling

4–8 oz (100–225 g) bacon	1 tablespoon flour
8 oz (225 g) cheese (preferably Gruyère but Cheddar is fine)	salt and pepper
	½ teaspoon grated nutmeg
4 eggs	¼ pint (1½ dl) single cream

To Make the Pastry

Sift together the flour and salt. Rub the butter into the flour, using the fingertips, until it is like coarse breadcrumbs. Add the water, all at once and mix. Knead lightly and set aside in a cool place or put in the refrigerator for 10–15 minutes. Roll it out.

68 It will cover a 9-inch (22 cm) dish, or a bigger one if you roll it out very thinly. Make sure you grease the tin. Prick the bottom of the pie with a fork. Place crumpled silver foil in the centre and bake 'blind' for 10 minutes in a hot oven (425°F, 220° C., Gas 7). If you use puff pastry, roll it out thinly and butter the pie dish well.

To Make the Filling

Fry the bacon and cut into small pieces. Grate the cheese. Beat together the eggs, flour, salt and pepper, nutmeg and cream. Fill the pastry case with alternate layers of cheese and bacon, starting and finishing with cheese. Pour over the egg and cream mixture and bake in a moderate oven (350°F, 180°C, Gas 4) for about 45 minutes until the custard is brown.

Onion or Leek Tart
Serves 6. Cooking time: 40 minutes

6 oz (150 g) shortcrust pastry or frozen puff pastry	4 oz (100 g) ham
	3 egg yolks
2 lb (1 kg) onions *or*	½ pint (3 dl) cream
2 lb (1 kg) leeks	salt and pepper
2 oz (50 g) butter or margarine	½ teaspoon grated nutmeg

Line a 9-inch (22 cm) greased pie dish with pastry, and bake 'blind', as for Quiche Lorraine. Cut the leeks down to an inch (2½ cm) of the white part. Wash thoroughly and slice finely. If using onions, peel and finely slice them. Fry, gently in butter, in a covered pan, until they are quite soft. Chop the ham and add to the vegetable mixture. Cook for a few minutes. Spoon this mixture into the pastry case. Beat together the egg yolks and cream and season with salt, pepper and nutmeg. Pour over the pie and bake in a hot oven (400°F, 200°C, Gas 6) until the filling is set, about 30 minutes.

Other vegetable tarts can be made in the same way as long as the vegetable has the moisture cooked out of it in the first place. You can have these prepared beforehand, pastry made, onions cooked, ready for quick final assembly and baking.

Kedgeree

Serves 6–8.   Cooking time: 20 minutes

Made with ingredients everyone has in their cupboard. Kedgeree is a great emergency meal.

1 lb (450 g) long grain rice
1 oz (25 g) butter
2 onions
1 heaped teaspoon curry powder

2 medium tins tuna (or use whatever fish you like)
2 eggs
chopped parsley
a dash of Worcester sauce

Peel and chop the onions. Flake the tuna with a fork. Boil the rice. Hardboil the eggs. Gently fry the chopped onions in the butter in a big pan until soft. Add the curry powder and cook for a minute or two. Drain the rice when it is *just* cooked. Chop up the eggs. Add the tuna, rice, eggs and parsley to the onions in the pan and as it is heating mix it and turn it gently, adding a little Worcester sauce.

Meat Sauce for Spaghetti
Serves 10–12.   Cooking time: 1 hour

'Everyone knows how to make *that*', they all said, and I suppose they are right, with spaghetti about as common now as peanut butter sandwiches. But you can't have a chapter called 'Weekend Food' without spaghetti so here is a very simple recipe.

2 lb (1 kg) minced steak
2 onions
1 clove garlic
1 dessertspoon tomato paste, or 4 oz (100 g) tomato purée or
   a few canned or fresh tomatoes
2 bay leaves
1 heaped teaspoon dried oregano
salt and pepper
stock cube

Peel and chop the onions. Crush the garlic. Fry the mince

until it is crumbly – you may not need to use the oil. Fry the onions and garlic in with the meat. Add all the other ingredients and enough water or stock *just* up to the level of the meat. Cover and simmer for at least 1 hour. It only takes a few minutes to heat, so if you can make it the day before, you can take the fat off easily.

It's worth shopping around for a good brand of spaghetti. Don't forget a spoonful of oil in the spaghetti cooking water. Finish cooking and drain while there is still that *tiny* uncooked centre as you bite.

Spaghetti di Mare
Serves 6. Cooking time: 25 minutes

More trouble than the previous spaghetti recipe but still very easy. For 1 lb (450 g) spaghetti you need:

1 lb (450 g) seafood – but more is much better – prawns, scallops (frozen will do), fish fillets steamed and cut in small pieces, whatever you like.
$\frac{1}{4}$–$\frac{1}{2}$ pint ($1\frac{1}{2}$–3 dl) single cream
$\frac{1}{2}$ glass dry white wine
2 tablespoons butter
3–4 tablespoons oil
1 clove garlic
salt and pepper
chopped parsley

Cook the fish. Chop the garlic. Cook and drain the spaghetti. Heat the garlic in the butter and oil and toss the spaghetti well with it. Add all the other ingredients, keeping the pan over medium heat and tossing everything through the spaghetti quickly in order to heat through.

The best ones I've made have been when I have had a little rich fish sauce to put on. If you cook scallops in butter first, or poach fish, boil down the liquid you have left and add it to the spaghetti. You get a richer, fishier flavour. It seems quite a lot of liquid I know, but spaghetti di mare needs to be well coated with sauce.

Puffed Potatoes

Serves 4–6.   Cooking time: 1 hour.   Allow 2 hours for soaking

2 lb (1 kg) new potatoes
salt

Halve medium-sized new potatoes lengthwise and soak them for several hours in very, very heavily salted water. Put them on an oven tray without drying them (cut side up) and into a very hot oven (450°F, 220°C, Gas 8) for 1 hour. The top will make a lovely brown bubble and everyone will immediately burst them to melt butter inside, but they are very pretty and very good. If you forget to soak them, they will usually puff if you just sprinkle them well with salt and let it dissolve before they go into the oven.

Marinade for Steak

Enough for 8.   Time taken: 3–4 hours

My children's favourite barbecue.

2 dessertspoons tomato purée   1 teaspoon sugar
1 dessertspoon Worcester sauce   1 clove garlic
1 teaspoon vinegar   salt and pepper
1 teaspoon olive oil

Crush the garlic and combine all the ingredients. Leave steak in the marinade for several hours, turning it over from time to time. I don't suggest you do this to a beautiful piece of rump steak; marinate the cheaper cuts it makes them full of flavour and very tender.

Marinade for Lamb Chops or Kebabs

Enough for 2 lb (1 kg) of meat.   Time taken: leave overnight

6 cloves garlic $\frac{1}{2}$ pint (3 dl) sour milk or yog-
3 onions   hurt
1 piece of fresh grated ginger   2 teaspoons curry paste
   or tinned ginger   salt and pepper

Crush the garlic. Peel the onions and chop or mince them. Combine all the ingredients. Leave meat in overnight. I have never actually used 6 cloves of garlic, but I give you the original recipe from the mother of a Swiss friend who is a marvellous cook.

Marinade for Pork Chops
Enough for 8 medium pork chops.   Time taken: Leave overnight

½ pint (3 dl) soya sauce
2 cloves garlic
1 tablespoon lemon juice

1 tablespoon chilli sauce
2 stock cubes
1 teaspoon olive oil

Crush the garlic. Mix together the ingredients. Cut most of the fat off the pork chops and marinate them overnight.

Marinade for Barbecued Chicken
Enough for 1 chicken.   Time taken: Leave overnight

¼ pint (1½ dl) olive oil
¼ pint (1½ dl) lemon juice
2 tablespoons finely chopped
  onion

1 teaspoon dried tarragon
salt and pepper

Mix together all the ingredients. Leave the chicken pieces in the marinade overnight. Barbecue the chicken slowly, turning and basting with the marinade. Even those miserable spring chickens or spatchcocks are good cooked like this, halved.

6. Favourite Cakes and Puddings

Cakes: Boiled Fruit Cake. Pineapple Boiled Fruit Cake. Chocolate Cake. Banana Cake. Gingerbread. Jenny's Special Coffee Cake. Chocolate Almond Cake. Butter Spongecake. Apple Cake. Upside Down Cake. Puddings: Apple Crumble. Pies: French Apple Tart. Pecan Pie. Raisin Pie. Baked Apples. Rice Pudding. Creme Caramel. Ride Croquettes. Pavlova (Neringue Case). Fruit Fool or Mousse.

I had almost given up cake-making since Jenny, my third daughter, started making cakes when she was about eight. She always wakes up extremely early, and can have a cake made, cooled (well, almost), iced (with candles added as the occasion arises), the cleaning up done and the cake brought up to our bed by quarter to seven. The bed gets a bit crumby but we eat it there and then on birthdays. I realize not everyone may feel like cake at 7 a.m. but I mention it as it is a culinary achievement unmatched by any other member of the family, particularly the cleaning up part. However, she has rather given up making cakes now, so it's back to me. I don't really mind as I find cake-making the most soothing of all cooking and recommend it for times of minor stress or even major catastrophe. It may take longer than counting to ten, but is much more calming.

I have only put in the recipes for the basic family cakes which cover everybody's favourite in this household. It was difficult to know what to do about puddings. Everyone's favourites again? But then someone said 'rice pudding' or 'baked apples' and when I said, 'but everyone knows how to make them,' the triumphant reply is, 'Well, why are they so terrible when we have them when we're out?' So they are in, and my apologies if you have been making perfect crème caramel and rice pudding all your life.

CAKES

Boiled Fruit Cake

Makes an 8-inch (20 cm) cake. Cooking time: 1½–2 hours. Allow extra time to cool

4 oz (100 g) butter	1 tablespoon lemon juice
8 oz (225 g) castor sugar	2 eggs
½ pint (3 dl) cold water	8 oz (225 g) self-raising flour
1½ lb (675 g) mixed dried fruit	8 oz (225 g) plain flour
1 teaspoon nutmeg	1 dessertspoon black treacle
1 teaspoon mixed spices	½ teaspoon bicarbonate of
(ginger, cinnamon etc.)	soda dissolved in
	1 tablespoon boiling water

Boil together the sugar, water, fruit, spices and lemon juice for 3 minutes. Add the butter and leave to cool. Beat the eggs well and add to the mixture, together with the treacle, flour and lastly the dissolved bicarbonate of soda. Turn into a lined and buttered tin, 8 inches (20 cm) square or round and fairly deep. Bake for about 1½–2 hours in a moderate oven (350°F, 180°C, Gas 4) decreasing heat after 1 hour. Test with skewer.

Pineapple Boiled Fruit Cake

Makes an 8-inch (20 cm) cake. Cooking time: 1½–2 hours. Allow extra time to cool

This is even nicer. Just substitute a 15 oz (375 g) tin of crushed pineapple for the water and ½ lb (225 g) of the fruit and proceed as for boiled fruit cake.

Chocolate Cake

Makes an 8-inch (20 cm) cake.   Cooking time: 25 minutes

Chocolate cake is everyone's favourite, and I must have tried more recipes for it than for anything else, and not been happy with the result. Here is yet another for you to try, I made it up (a thing I seldom do) and it makes a slightly sticky cake, which is preferable to that most dreaded thing, a dry chocolate cake. It probably keeps very well. I never have a chance to find out for you. I wish I could find one as good made with cocoa instead of chocolate, which would be cheaper.

4 oz (100 g) cooking chocolate
4 oz (100 g) butter or margarine (softened)
12 oz (350 g) brown sugar (loosely packed)
1 teaspoon vanilla essence
3 eggs (separated)
1 lb (450 g) plain flour
½ pint (3 dl) milk
1 teaspoon bicarbonate of soda dissolved in 1 tablespoon boiling water
¼–½ pint (1½–3 dl) double cream

Melt the chocolate gently (it hardly needs any heat) and beat it with the butter, sugar, vanilla and egg yolks with an electric mixer if you have one. Blend in the flour and milk alternately. Fold in the stiffly beaten egg whites – gently, but fold them *right* in, and last the soda dissolved in the boiling water. It looks a bit runnier than you would be happy about. Pour into 2 prepared 8-inch (20 cm) tins (buttered and lined) and cook in a hot oven (400°F, 200°C, Gas 6) for 25 minutes. Watch carefully to see it does not overcook, test with a skewer or take it out as soon as that damp look has disappeared from the top. Cool and put together with whipped cream and ice with chocolate icing.

For the Icing

3 oz (75 g) plain, block chocolate
4 tablespoons water

8 oz (225 g) icing sugar
2–3 drops vanilla essence

Break the chocolate into small pieces and put in a saucepan with the water. Dissolve over low heat and bring to the boil. Cool slightly. Stir in the sieved icing sugar and add the vanilla essence.

Banana Cake

Makes a 7-inch (18 cm) cake.   Cooking time: 20–25 minutes

For using up those bananas no one will eat.

4 oz (100 g) margarine
8 oz (225 g) castor sugar
2 eggs
3 bananas
1 lb (450 g) self-raising flour

1 level teaspoon bicarbonate of soda
3 tablespoons milk
1 teaspoon vanilla essence

Cream margarine and sugar. Add beaten eggs, then mashed bananas and vanilla. Sift in flour and soda alternately with milk. This makes two 7-inch (18 cm) sandwich tins (buttered and lined) or one large square tin. Cook for 20–25 minutes in a moderate oven (350°F, 180°C, Gas 4) or until done when tested with a skewer. Ice with lemon icing.

For the Icing

8 oz (225 g) icing sugar
1 oz (25 g) butter

2 tablespoons milk
$\frac{1}{4}$ teaspoon lemon juice

Put milk, butter and lemon juice into a saucepan over gentle heat until butter has melted. Sift icing sugar into a bowl. Pour in liquid and mix.

Jenny's Special Coffee Cake

Makes an 8-inch (20 cm) cake.   Cooking time: 25 minutes

4 oz (100 g) margarine
4 oz (100 g) castor sugar
2 eggs

4 oz (100 g) self-raising flour
2 teaspoons coffee essence or strong black coffee

Cream margarine and sugar, beat in the eggs and coffee, fold in the sifted flour. Bake in a greased and floured 8-inch (20 cm) cake tin in a moderate oven (250°F, 180°C, Gas 4) for 25 minutes. Turn out and when cool, ice with the following icing.

For the Icing

3 oz (75 g) icing sugar	1 oz (25 g) sugar
1 oz (25 g) butter	1 teaspoon coffee essence
1 tablespoon boiling water	

Boil together the butter, water and sugar. Pour this mixture over the sifted icing sugar, add the coffee essence and beat well. When cold, beat until light and spread on cake. Decorate as the occasion demands.

Gingerbread

Makes an 8-inch (20 cm) cake. Cooking time: 1 hour. Allow extra time to cool

4 oz (100 g) butter or margarine	2 eggs
	1 lb (450 g) plain flour
4 oz (100 g) black treacle (weigh on floured scales to avoid sticking)	1 teaspoon mixed spice
	1 tablespoon ground ginger
	1 teaspoon bicarbonate of soda
2 oz (50 g) golden syrup	
¼ pint (1½ dl) milk	¼ teaspoon salt

Heat butter, treacle, golden syrup and milk gently until they are blended. Cool. Add well beaten eggs. Sift the dry ingredients into a bowl. Slowly add the liquid, mixing well. Pour into a buttered 8-inch (20 cm) square tin. Bake in a slow oven (300°F, 150°C, Gas 2) for about 1 hour. Ice with lemon icing when cold (see page 00).

I always make a double quantity of this and have half hot for pudding, with custard or ice cream.

Chocolate Almond Cake

Makes 8-inch (20cm) cake. Cooking ime: 30 minutes. Allow extra time to cool

Very easy, very rich, and grand enough for a dinner party dessert.

4 eggs separated	4 oz (100 g) dark chocolate
4 tablespoons castor sugar	4 oz (100 g) ground almonds

Melt the chocolate over very low heat or in a double boiler. Beat the egg yolks and sugar until light. Add the melted chocolate and then the ground almonds. Beat egg whites stiffly and fold in thoroughly. Pour into a buttered spring-form pan and bake in a moderate oven (375°F, 190° C, Gas 5) for approximately 30 minutes (test with skewer). Cool and cover with topping.

Topping

$\frac{1}{4}$ pint ($1\frac{1}{2}$ dl) whipped cream
4 oz (100 g) dark chocolate

Melt and slightly cool the chocolate, then swirl it into the cream and on to the cake. Do not mix the chocolate and cream, just get a marbled effect. Store the cake in the refrigerator so that the chocolate in the topping sets again.

Butter Spongecake

Makes 9-inch (22 cm) cake.   Cooking time: 30 minutes

2 oz (50 g) butter
4 eggs (separated)
4 oz (100 g) castor sugar
2 extra tablespoons castor
  sugar

2 teaspoons vanilla essence
$3\frac{1}{2}$ oz (87 g) self-raising flour
pinch salt

Melt butter and leave to cool. Turn oven to (350°F, 180°C, Gas 4). Butter and flour a deep 9-inch (22 cm) round cake tin.

Beat the egg yolks with the vanilla and 4 oz (100 g) castor sugar until pale and thick. In another bowl beat the egg whites with a pinch of salt until soft peaks form, add the extra 2 tablespoons castor sugar and continue beating until stiff peaks are formed. Sift the flour three times. Fold the egg whites and sifted flour into the egg yolks, a quarter of each at a time, not mixing completely each time. Finally fold in the melted butter (not the white residue at the bottom). Be careful not to overmix.

Turn into the cake tin and tip it so that the mixture runs
into the rim all around. It will look disastrous but it does work.
Bake for 30 minutes, or when cake shrinks slightly from tin.
Cool for a few minutes before loosening around edges with a
knife and turning on to a cake-rack.

For the Filling

strawberry jam
$\frac{1}{4}$ pint ($1\frac{1}{2}$ dl) double cream
icing sugar

Reverse, cool and fill with strawberry jam and whipped
cream. Sift icing sugar over the top.

Apple Cake

Makes an 8-inch (20 cm) cake.   Cooking time: 35 minutes.
Allow extra time if stewing fruit

12 oz (300 g) of fairly dry stewed fruit (apples, prunes, dried
apricots or any other stewed fruit as long as it's not too juicy)

4 oz (100 g) butter or   1 tablespoon iced water
   margarine $\frac{1}{2}$ lb (225 g) self-raising flour
6 oz (174 g) castor sugar
1 egg

Cream butter and sugar, beat in the egg then the water and
sifted flour. It is more like soft pastry dough than cake mixture.
Butter an 8-inch (20 cm) round cake tin. Take a little over half
the mixture and pat it out in the bottom of the tin and slightly
up the sides. You will need to flour your fingers. Add the fruit
and pat the rest of the mixture over the top. It doesn't matter
if it looks very ragged. Bake in a moderate oven (375°F,
190°C, Gas 5) for 35 minutes. It turns out easily and is delicious,
especially if you've used prunes. Serve slightly warm or cold,
with whipped cream. If you use brown sugar instead of white,
it is much crunchier.

Upside Down Cake

Makes an 8-inch (20 cm) cake.   Cooking time: 35 minutes. Allow extra time if stewing fruit

2 tablespoons brown sugar
12 oz (350 g) stewed and drained dried apricots or prunes (or any fruit you like)
2 oz (50 g) butter or margarine
1 (extra) oz (25 g) butter
2½ tablespoons castor sugar
1 egg
12 oz (350 g) self-raising flour
¼ pint (1½ dl) milk

Melt the extra ounce of butter with the brown sugar. Pour this into the base of an 8-inch (20 cm) cake tin. Spoon the fruit over this. Cream butter and sugar, beat in the egg, then the flour and milk alternately. Spread over the fruit. Bake in a moderate oven (375°F, 190°C, Gas 5) for 25 minutes. Turn out on a plate and serve hot with cream, ice cream or custard.

PUDDINGS

Most of us don't make puddings every day as our mothers did, but here are my favourite family ones, some *very* quick. First of all, crumble topping, which you can make in about one minute. It goes over any fruit you may have, and is practically every child's favourite pudding.

Apple Crumble

Makes enough to fill an 11-inch (26 cm) dish.   Cooking time: 30 minutes

6 oz (175 g) self-raising flour   3 tablespoons coconut
3 tablespoons brown or white sugar   2 oz (50 g) butter

Rub the butter into the rest of the ingredients until crumbly. Put stewed apples (or other stewed, bottled or tinned fruit) into a pie dish and sprinkle topping over them. Bake for about 30 minutes in a moderate oven (350°F, 180°C, Gas 4) until brown. Serve with whipped cream, ice cream or custard. Good hot or cold.

I use those ready-made, ready-baked, pastry cases for these family pies and only some sort of vanity stops me using them for guests as they are perfectly good for pies in which the filling is cooked *in* the pastry case.

French Apple Tart
Fills 2 ready-baked 6-inch (16 cm) pastry cases or an 8–9-inch (20–22 cm) tin. Cooking time: 35–45 minutes. Allow extra time if you make the pastry

Why French? I don't know, but that's what we've always called it. You can make it with peaches too.

4 cooking apples
5 level tablespoons castor sugar
2½ tablespoons plain flour

1 teaspoon cinnamon
1 teaspoon nutmeg
½ pint (3 dl) double cream

Peel, core and finely slice the apples. Put them in a large bowl and toss the dry ingredients through them with 2 forks. Tip into the pastry cases and pour the cream over. Bake for 35–40 minutes in a hot oven (400°F, 200°C, Gas 6). Let them cool a little before serving. They can be served cold but are best just warm.

Pecan Pie
Fills 2 ready-baked 6-inch (16 cm) pastry cases. Cooking time: Or an 8–9 inch (20–22 cm) tin   30 minutes.

If you can get pecans, otherwise substitute walnuts.

2 oz (50 g) butter
6 oz (175 g) brown sugar
3 eggs
8 oz (225 g) golden syrup

8 oz (225 g) chopped pecans
  or walnuts
1 tablespoon vanilla essence
¼ teaspoon salt

Cream butter and sugar. Beat in eggs. Stir in the other ingredients. Pour into pie shells. Bake in a moderate oven (375°F, 190°F, Gas 5) for 30 minutes. Serve hot or cold, with cream or ice cream.

Vermont Raisin Pie
Fills 2 ready-made 6-inch (16 cm) pastry cases.   Cooking time:
Or *an 8–9-inch (20–22 cm) tin*   *45 minutes.*

1 tablespoon plain flour
½ teaspoon ground cinnamon
¼ teaspoon ground nutmeg
¼ teaspoon salt
6 oz (175 g) castor sugar

2 egg yolks
¼ pint (1½ dl) milk
1 carton sour cream
6 oz (175 g) seedless raisins

Blend dry ingredients, stir in egg yolks, then milk, sour cream and raisins. Pour into shells and bake in a moderate oven (365°F, 190°C, Gas 5) for 45 minutes. The filling sets more as it cools. Serve slightly warm or cold.

Baked Apples
Serves 4.   Cooking time: 1 hour

dates or sultanas
4 cooking apples

4 oz (100 g) brown sugar
butter

Core apples and cut just through the skin in a ring around the middle to stop them bursting. Stand in an ovenproof dish and stuff the centre with dates or sultanas. Put a nut of butter on the top of each. Dissolve the sugar in a cup of hot water and pour around the apples. Bake in a moderate oven (350°F, 180°C, Gas 4) until soft but not falling to bits. Serve hot with cream or custard.

Rice Pudding
Serves 4–6.   Cooking time: 3 hours

The only way to make good plain rice pudding is to cook it slowly for a long time. Three hours in a slow oven is not too much.

2 oz (50 g) round grain rice
1 pint (6 dl) milk

1 dessertspoon sugar
vanilla essence

Butter a pie dish well. Put in the rice and sugar, pour over the milk, add vanilla essence and stir. Cook in a slow oven (275°F, 140°C, Gas 1) for 3 hours, stirring occasionally at first so that the grains do not stick together. Don't stir for the last hour or so, in order to get a nice brown skin.

Crème Caramel
Serves 4–6. Cooking time: 45–50 minutes

So many recipes for crème caramel call for cream instead of milk but it is not really necessary. All that is necessary is to take great care to get it out of the oven when the custard has *just* set and is still pretty wobbly. It gets firmer as it cools. And do not let the water in the surrounding tin boil or there will be holes in the custard.

The Caramel

3 tablespoons sugar
1 tablespoon water

Put the sugar in a small saucepan with the water. Melt and bring to the boil, swirling it around a bit, but not stirring. Boil until it caramelizes, don't let it get too dark, just amber-coloured. Pour it quickly into a mould (a pyrex dish is fine) and tip it around to cover the base and sides, or as much of the sides as you can before it sets.

The Custard

4 eggs   vanilla essence
2 tablespoons castor sugar   1 pint (6 dl) milk

Beat together the eggs, sugar and vanilla. Scald the milk and pour on to the egg mixture. Stir. Strain it into the caramel-lined mould and stand the mould in a pan of hot water. Cover with a piece of paper and cook in a moderate oven (350°F, 180°C, Gas 4) until the custard has just set – 45 minutes, but you must watch to see if this is right for you. It varies a bit with depth of bowl, height of water in pan surrounding and so on. Cool. Chill. Turn out when cold.

Rice Croquettes

Makes 14 fairly large croquettes.   Cooking time: 60–70 minutes

These really are quite messy to make but there was such an outcry from my own family when I said I wasn't putting them in that I relented. As with any recipe which takes much time – I do it in stages, when you have a spare moment.

8 oz (225 g) pudding rice	1 egg white (lightly beaten)
1 pint (6 dl) milk	2 tablespoons cream
4 level tablespoons sugar	apricot jam
piece of vanilla pod	flour
nut of butter	ground almonds or
3 egg yolks	breadcrumbs
	oil for frying

Wash the rice, cover with cold water and bring to boil. Take off stove and let it stand for 5 minutes. Drain and rinse under cold running water. Return to pan with sugar, vanilla pod and milk. Bring to boil, add butter, turn down heat to very low, cover the pan and cook until rice is tender – about 45 minutes depending on how low you can get the burner on your stove. Take off heat. Beat the egg yolks with the cream and mix into the rice well with a fork. Turn the rice out on to a plate and leave to cool. Later on, make into balls, with a small teaspoon of apricot jam in the centre. Roll the balls in flour, dip in lightly beaten egg white and coat with either chopped almonds (best) or fine dry breadcrumbs. Put in refrigerator until time to cook. Fry in very hot oil, turning once carefully. They would be better smaller if you are clever at this sort of thing. Serve hot, with whipped cream.

Pavlova (Meringue Case)

Serves 6–8.   Cooking time: 1½ hours

For all those egg whites, if you make as much mayonnaise as I do. (Egg whites keep perfectly well in a covered jar in the refrigerator – for at least a week.)

4 egg whites	1 teaspoon vinegar
8 oz (225 g) castor sugar	1 level tablespoon cornflour
1 teaspoon vanilla essence	

Beat egg whites until stiff. Beat in castor sugar gradually until
very stiff and glossy (much easier if you have an electric beater
with a whisk). Fold in the vanilla, vinegar and cornflour. Put
a sheet of aluminium foil on an oven tray and spread the
meringue on it in a circle, building it up around the edges if
you like. It will spread and puff up a bit. Bake in a very slow
oven (250°F, 130°C, Gas ½) for 1½ hours. You should have a
thin outside layer of crisp meringue with a marshmallow centre.
It might crack a bit as it cools, which makes it hard to turn
upside down when trying to peel off the foil. Cover it with
whipped cream and fruit.

Fruit Fool or Mousse
Serves 6–8.   Time taken: 20 minutes.   Allow extra time to chill

Not everyone likes these creamy desserts, but they are my
favourites, next to a really beautifully baked custard. Strawberries make the best but only when they are very fresh and full
of flavour – if you can smell the strawberries as you walk past
the greengrocer that's the day for strawberry mousse. Rasp-
berries are good, so are stewed dried apricots (with a little
grated orange rind added and slivered almonds if you like)
equally, stewed rhubarb or stewed gooseberries.

1 pint (6 dl) double cream
1 pint (6 dl) puréed fruit (if using cooked fruit use very little
    water in the cooking)
6 oz (175 g) castor sugar and 1 tablespoon lemon juice stirred
    into the fruit until dissolved. If you have sugared the stewed
    fruit you would not use this much, of course
2 teaspoons–2 dessertspoons powdered gelatine
⅛ pint (¾ dl) water

Soak the gelatine in the water and warm to dissolve. You need
the larger amount if you want to unmould it, but I think the
smaller amount gives a better consistency. Cool the gelatine
and add to the fruit and when it starts to thicken fold in the
beaten cream. Pile in a glass serving bowl or mould. Chill for
several hours or overnight.

7. Cooking for Presents

Tuna Pâtè. Tarragon Butter. Pesto. Green Tomato Pickle with Beans. Rum Balls. Apricot Balls. Sherried Cherries. Western Sunset Savoury Biscuits. Cheese Marbles. Mince-meat. Brandy Butter. Christmas Pudding with Suet. Christmas Pudding with Butter. Christmas Cake.

Cooking for presents is a nice warm thing to do and it can also take care of those difficult times when you can't think what to give someone – after all, everyone likes food. One Mother's Day I gave my mother-in-law three ovenproof dishes, one filled with mayonnaise, one with pâté and one with béarnaise sauce and she loved it. Another successful venture was tarragon butter, packed in those nice little individual brown butter pots. This was one year when good tarragon was impossible to buy and I had been sent some packets of the dried that was very good. When I have lots of basil growing I make pesto, that best of all Italian sauces for pasta, because hardly anyone seems to make that for themselves.

Kipper pâté is on page 57. Here is a good tuna pâté as well.

Will fit into a small terrine. Time taken: 15 minutes. 10 minutes (with blender). Allow extra time to chill

1 lb (450 g) tinned tuna (tinned in oil)
8 oz (225 g) softened butter
4–6 tablespoons olive oil
juice of 1 lemon
1 teaspoon dried mustard
2 level tablespoons grated onion (if using a blender, you need not grate it)
salt and pepper
2 tablespoons brandy (I like it better without the brandy)

Pound all ingredients together, or combine in the blender. Pack into a small terrine or 2 smaller pots and chill.

Tarragon Butter
Makes 4 oz (100 g) butter. Time taken: 15 minutes

1 tablespoon fresh, chopped tarragon leaves (or very good dried tarragon)
4 oz (100 g) butter
freshly ground pepper
squeeze of lemon juice

Pound together the tarragon and butter, with the pepper and lemon juice. Pack into small pots. Tarragon butter can be frozen.

Pesto
Time taken: 20 minutes

You need 2 oz (50 g) of basil, after removing the stems. This is quite a lot, so it is really for people who grow it themselves. It is fairly easy to grow however and once you have grown it, neither a summer nor a tomato will ever seem the same without it. It grows well in pots.

The rest of the ingredients are:

2 cloves garlic

1 oz (25 g) pine nuts

1 oz (25 g) parmesan cheese

salt

4–5 tablespoons olive oil

Everything except the olive oil must be pounded together in a mortar until it is a thick purée. The oil is then added slowly, beating all the time, making sure the oil is absorbed before adding more. The finished sauce should have the consistency of creamed butter. Make sure the people to whom you're giving it know what it is and how to use it. In fact, I think it's always better to label everything.

Green Tomato Pickle with Beans

Cooking time: 45 minutes.   Leave overnight

This pickle is very good with cold meat or for sandwiches, and nothing like bought pickle.

6 lb (3 kg) green tomatoes

2 lb (1 kg) onions

2 lb (1 kg) runner or haricot vert beans

2½ lb (1¼ kg) white sugar

1 tablespoon peppercorns

1 tablespoon whole cloves

} tied in a bag

1 tablespoon dry mustard

1 tablespoon tumeric

2 tablespoons flour

8 oz (225 g) salt

vinegar

Halve tomatoes and slice thinly. Cut beans in small thin pieces. Mix. Sprinkle the salt over them and stand overnight. Next day drain off the liquid and put tomatoes and beans in a big pan. Peel and finely slice the onions. Put in the same pan, together with sugar, pepper and cloves. Almost cover with vinegar. Boil for 30 minutes.

Mix mustard, flour and tumeric to a thin paste with a little vinegar, add it to the pan and boil for a further 15 minutes. Bottle, cover and label.

Christmas time is the best time of all for present cooking. It's a nice festive thing to do with your children, they love it, and perhaps you will be feeling so goodwillish that the mess they make won't seem as bad as at other times. It is good if you can steer the children towards acceptable cooking, so that it won't be *only* the thought that counts, although I know it's hard to convince some people that Gran may not love toffees with hundreds and thousands on top.

My children collect screwtop jars at Christmas time and paint the lids and wobbly holly on them. Not that there's anything very original about that, I did the same and you probably did too. Here are some of the children's Christmas present recipes, most of which came from my mother. All this rolling into balls would drive me crazy but the children like it.

Rum Balls
Time taken: 40 minutes

8 oz (225 g) tin sweetened condensed milk
8 oz (225 g) plain crushed biscuits

8 oz (225 g) coconut
2 tablespoons cocoa
3 dessertspoons rum

Mix all ingredients together well. Make into small balls. Roll in coconut. Store in screwtop jar in refrigerator.

Apricot Balls
Time taken: 30 minutes

12 oz (350 g) dried apricots, minced or chopped up finely
1¼ lb (550 g) coconut
1/3 pint (2 dl) sweetened condensed milk
icing sugar

Mix all ingredients together well. Form into balls and roll in icing sugar. Store in refrigerator.

Sherried Cherries
Time taken: 40 minutes.   Leave overnight

crystallized cherries
4 oz (100 g) melted butter
12 oz (350 g) icing sugar

12 oz (350 g) coconut
few drops of almond essence

Soak some crystallized cherries overnight in sweet sherry (or something else – Kirsch, marsala, whatever you have).

Mix the butter, icing sugar and almond essence. Form into balls with a cherry in the middle. This is easier than you might imagine as the mixture is quite soft. Roll in coconut and store in refrigerator.

Here are some cheese biscuits one of the children made last Christmas with great success.

Western Sunset Savoury Biscuits
Will fit into an 8-inch (20 cm) tin.   Time taken: 1 hour

They are given that strange name by one of my sisters. She lives in the outback of Australia where the sunsets are spectacular. What that had to do with naming her excellent cheese biscuits I don't know.

2 bacon rashers
4 oz (100 g) soft butter or
  margarine
8 oz (225 g) grated cheese
  (choose a fairly strong one)

8 oz (225 g) self-raising flour
1 teaspoon salt
$\frac{1}{4}$ teaspoon cayenne pepper

Fry the bacon until crisp. Cut into small pieces. Combine the ingredients in the order given and mix well. Press into an 8-inch (20 cm) square tin and mark into small squares with a sharp knife. Bake in a moderate oven (350°F, 180°C, Gas 4) until golden brown. Allow to cool in the tin. Divide into squares and store in an airtight container.

Cheese Marbles

Time taken: 50 minutes

4 oz (100 g) butter
6 oz (150 g) self-raising flour
6 oz (150 g) grated cheese (choose a fairly strong one)
salt, cayenne pepper
coconut

Melt the butter, mix in the flour, salt and cayenne. Work in the cheese to a stiff paste. Break off pieces and roll into balls. Roll in coconut. Place on greased tray and bake in a moderate oven (350°F, 180°C, Gas 4) for 20 minutes or until golden.

Jars of mincemeat and brandy butter make good presents, as do homemade Christmas cakes or puddings – though they're expensive. You probably have masses of recipes for them, here are some more for you to choose from.

Mincemeat

Makes 7 ($\frac{1}{2}$ lb) (225 g) jars.   Time taken: 30–40 minutes

This one is minced, rather than leaving the fruit whole, but you could do it either way.

6 large cooking apples
1 lb (450 g) raisins
1 lb (450 g) sultanas
8 oz (225 g) currants

4 oz (100 g) whole candied peel
4 oz (100 g) dried apricots
12 oz (350 g) suet (or use packet suet, preparing suet is awful)

Peel and core the apples. Mince the other ingredients coarsely. Then add:

2 oz (50 g) blanched, skinned and chopped almonds
$\frac{1}{2}$ grated nutmeg
$\frac{1}{2}$ teaspoon mace
$\frac{1}{2}$ teaspoon cinnamon

$\frac{1}{4}$ pint ($1\frac{1}{2}$ dl) brandy
1 lb (450 g) sugar
grated rind and juice of 1 lemon

Mix well and pack in jars. It is very thick and makes marvellous mince pies, but leave the fruit whole (chop apricots and apples) if you don't think you would like it this way.

Brandy Butter
Makes about 1 lb (450 g).   Time taken: 15–20 minutes

8 oz (225 g) butter (unsalted for preference but need not be)
8 oz (225 g) icing sugar

4–5 tablespoons brandy
little grated nutmeg

Cream together the softened butter and icing sugar until light. Add a sprinkling of nutmeg and beat in the brandy gradually. This may seem a lot of brandy (only use cheap brandy of course) but it needs a lot. It may even hold a little more without curdling. It will now be very light and fluffy. Put into bowls to harden and store in the refrigerator.

Christmas Pudding with Suet
Makes two 4-pint (2·4) litre) puddings.   Cooking time: 6 hours. Plus 2 hours on the day.   Leave overnight

This recipe, as you will see, has brandy, sherry, stout and rum in it. I always use them all, partly because it seems so ridiculous. I'm sure the variety is not essential.

1 lb (450 g) sultanas
12 oz (325 g) raisins
10 oz (250 g) mixed peel
2 oz (50 g) chopped, dried, apricots
2 oz (50 g) glacé cherries

2 oz (50 g) blanched, chopped almonds
grated rind of 1 lemon
1 tablespoon spices (nutmeg, cinnamon, cloves, ginger)
2 tablespoons each brandy, sherry and rum

Mix all these together and stand overnight.

6 oz (150 g) brown sugar
8 oz (225 g) plain flour
1 teaspoon baking powder

10 oz (250 g) finely grated suet (out of a packet, or get your
    butcher to do it for you)
1½ lb (675 g) soft, white, breadcrumbs
4 eggs
½ pint (3 dl) stout

Combine everything except the eggs and stout and add the
fruit mixture to them. Beat the eggs, add the stout, mix in
well. Steam for 6 hours and a further 2 on the day of serving.
For presents, a 2-pint (12 dl) basin makes a nice pudding,
serving 6 easily, or you could make it into 3 smaller ones. I
always boil puddings in ordinary china basins, buttered and
covered with buttered paper and then brown paper or foil.
Halve the cooking time if you divide the mixture between two
bowls.

Christmas Pudding with Butter

Makes two 4pint (2·4) litre puddings.   Cooking time: 5 hours.
Plus 2 hours on the day.   Allow 1 week for soaking

1 lb (450 g) sultanas
1 lb (450 g) chopped raisins
8 oz (225 g) chopped peel
1 dozen large prunes
grated rind of 1 orange and
    1 lemon
4 oz (100 g) blanched,
    chopped, almonds
4 tablespoons rum
8 oz (225 g) butter
5 eggs

8 oz (225 g) dark brown sugar
1 tablespoon black treacle
1 mashed banana
½ pint (3 dl) milk
½ lb (225 g) plain flour
1 teaspoon bicarbonate of
    soda
1 tablespoon mixed spices
½ teaspoon salt
½ teaspoon ground cloves
½ lb (225 g) breadcrumbs

Soak the fruit and almonds in the rum for a week. Cream butter
and sugar, beat in eggs. Add treacle and mashed banana. Sift
flour, soda, salt, spices and stir in. Add the milk, then the
breadcrumbs, then the fruit.
    Butter and flour 2 basins, fill to two thirds, cover with
buttered paper and foil and tie down firmly. Steam for 5 hours,

keep for a couple of months if possible. Steam for another 2 hours on the day.

Christmas Cake
Makes 1 (9-inch) (22 cm) cake or 2 or 3 (6-inch) (16 cm) cakes.
Cooking time: 3 hours (for large). 1½ hours (for small).
Leave overnight

8 oz (225 g) raisins	8 oz (225 g) butter
8 oz (225 g) sultanas	8 oz (225 g) dark brown sugar
4 oz (100 g) peel	5 large eggs
4 oz (100 g) glacé cherries	1 rounded tablespoon plum jam
4 oz (100 g) glacé or crystallized pineapple	10 oz (250 g) plain flour
4 oz (100 g) blanched, chopped, almonds	½ level teaspoon bicarbonate of soda
4 tablespoons brandy or rum	¼ level teaspoon salt
8 oz (225 g) stoned prunes	2 oz (50 g) ground almonds
grated rind 1 lemon	

Mix fruit (not prunes) and chopped almonds, sprinkle with brandy or rum and stand overnight (covered).

Cream butter, lemon rind and sugar, beat in eggs one at a time, then add plum jam and minced or finely cut up prunes. Add the sifted flour, soda and salt in halves, mixing well. Mix in the ground almonds, then the fruit in halves. Line tins with greased foil or greased paper. Start in a moderate oven (350°F, 180°C, Gas 4) reduce to slow after about an hour (300°F, 150°C, Gas 2). Be very careful not to overcook. Sprinkle with a little more rum or brandy when hot from the oven.

Index